Principles of Costing

Tutorial

Aubrey Penning

Published by Osborne Books Limited
Unit 1B Everoak Estate
Bromyard Road
Worcester WR2 5HP
Tel 01905 748071
Email books@osbornebooks.co.uk
Website www.osbornebooks.co.uk

Design by Laura Ingham

Printed by CPI Group (UK) Limited, Croydon, CR0 4YY, on environmentally friendly, acid-free paper from managed forests.

British Library Cataloguing in Publication Data
A catalogue record for this book is available from the British Library

ISBN 978-1-911198-54-3

Contents

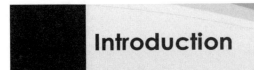

Introduction

Qualifications covered

This book has been written specifically to cover the Unit 'Principles of costing' which is mandatory for the following qualifications:

AAT Level 2 Certificate in Accounting

AAT Level 2 Certificate in Bookkeeping

AAT Certificate in Accounting – SCQF Level 6

The book contains a clear text with worked examples and case studies, chapter summaries and key terms to help with revision. Each chapter concludes with a wide range of activities, many in the style of AAT computer based assessments.

Osborne Study and Revision Materials

Additional materials, tailored to the needs of students studying this unit and revising for the assessment, include:

- **Workbooks:** paperback books with practice activities and exams
- **Wise Guides:** pocket-sized spiral bound revision cards
- **Student Zone:** access to Osborne Books online resources
- **Osborne Books App:** Osborne Books ebooks for mobiles and tablets

Visit www.osbornebooks.co.uk for details of study and revision resources and access to online material.

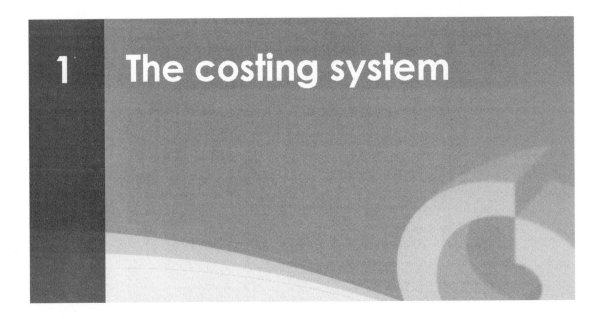

1 The costing system

this chapter covers...

In this chapter we introduce costing by discussing what costing is, and then learn about some of the techniques that are used in costing.

We will start by explaining that the purpose of costing is to provide information for managers about costs and income in a range of organisations and situations. This will help managers to set selling prices, value inventory (stock), and make decisions.

We will then examine how costing systems are developed to match the organisation and its information needs. There are many different types of organisation, carrying out different activities in different ways, and the costing system needs to be able to produce the information that is most useful to manage the organisation.

Costing is part of management accounting and costing information is produced for those inside the business with a view to managing the future.

The next step is to see where the data that can be used for costing can be found. Calculations of current and future costs make use of the financial records (past 'historic' data) and also present day information and forecasts.

We will complete the chapter by showing how costs can be grouped together, or classified in several ways. The first is to divide costs into their elements – materials, labour and expenses. We can also classify costs based on their purpose or 'function', and by their 'nature'.

Once you have finished studying this chapter you should have a clear idea about why costing is needed, and appreciate some of the ideas that it uses.

PURPOSE OF COSTING

Costing (or 'cost accounting' to give its more formal name) enables the managers of a business to know the cost of the firm's output – whether a product or a service – and the revenues from sales. Once costing information is available, managers can use it to assist with decision making, planning for the future and the control of expenditure.

Cost accounting is widely used by:

■ a **manufacturing business** which makes a product, eg a car

■ a **business** that provides a service, eg a holiday company

A business – whether a manufacturer or a service provider – needs to keep its costs under review. In order to do this it needs accurate **cost information**. A cost accounting system will provide answers to questions such as:

What does it cost us to provide a student with a day's accountancy course?

What does it cost us to carry out a hip replacement operation?

What does it cost us to make a pair of trainers?

What does it cost us to serve a cheeseburger and fries?

What does it cost us to provide a week's holiday in the Canaries?

By being able to work out the cost of a product or service, the managers of an organisation can then use this cost to:

■ help **determine a selling price** (which of course needs to be higher than cost in order to make a profit)

■ **value inventory** (stock) that the organisation holds

■ provide **information for financial statements**

■ **make management decisions** (for example about how many items should be made and sold)

These are the key purposes of a costing system.

WHAT IS A COSTING SYSTEM?

A costing system is used by an organisation to collect information about costs and use that information for decision making, planning and control.

Every organisation can develop its own costing system to suit itself – what is important is the type of information it wants to get from the system, and this will determine how the system works. Costing systems could be:

- very simple – for example a series of written cost calculations for its products, or
- very complex – for example a computerised system that provides a range of reports that compare actual costs with expected costs and analyses the differences

The costing system that an organisation uses will need some 'rules' so that everyone using the system will do things in the same way. It would not be very useful if one product's cost was calculated in one way while another product's cost was worked out by an entirely different method. These 'rules' would be set up by the organisation – there are no legal or other external requirements that force organisations to carry out their costing in a particular way.

costing in different organisations

As already mentioned, costing systems will be different for different organisations. We have already seen that organisations as different as hospitals and holiday companies will need to have a costing system that suits their needs. We will show how a costing system divides up or classifies costs into various categories to make the information about costs more useful.

This **classification of costs** will also be different depending on the organisation and what it does, for example a hairdresser and a garage that sells cars.

FINANCIAL ACCOUNTING AND MANAGEMENT ACCOUNTING

Much of your accounting studies will be based on '**financial accounting**' where ledgers and other books and records are used to record financial transactions. If you study the basics of accounting you are likely to look first at bookkeeping. Although some of the information that is used in a costing system will come from the financial accounting ledgers, the costing system is usually quite separate, and has distinctly different purposes as we have already noted – to help with decision making, planning and control.

Costing is part of a larger area of study called '**management accounting**', which also includes topics such as budgeting and analysing the performance of a business or other organisation.

The following simple diagram illustrates the relationship between financial and management accounting.

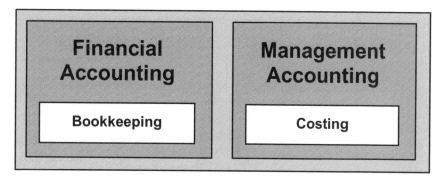

We will now examine the relationship between these two types of accounting in more detail.

what is financial accounting?

Financial accounting is concerned with recording financial transactions that have happened already, and with providing information from the accounting records – for example in order to prepare VAT returns, and the financial statements of a business.

The main features of financial accounting are that it:

- records transactions that have happened already

- looks back to show what has happened in the past

- is accurate to the nearest penny, with no estimated amounts

- is often a legal requirement to keep accounts (for example in order to prepare VAT returns)

- maintains confidentiality of information (eg payroll details, VAT returns)

what is management accounting?

Management accounting (including costing) is concerned with looking at actual transactions in different ways from financial accounting. In particular, the costs of each product or service are considered both in the past and as the likely costs in the future.

In this way, management accounting is able to provide information to help the business or organisation plan for the future.

The main features of management accounting are that it:

- uses accounting information to summarise transactions that have happened already and to make estimates for the future

- looks in detail at the costs and the sales income of products and services
- looks forward to show what is likely to happen in the future
- may use estimates where these are the most suitable form of information
- provides management with reports that are of use in running the business or organisation
- provides management information as frequently as circumstances demand – speed is often vital as information may go out-of-date very quickly
- is not usually sent to people outside the organisation – it is for internal use
- maintains confidentiality of information (eg payroll details)

A detailed summary of the differences between financial and cost accounting is illustrated in the diagram below.

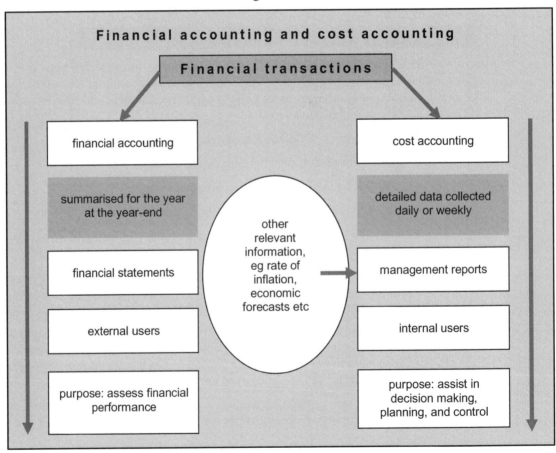

SOURCES OF DATA FOR COSTING

We saw in the last section how financial accounting has a different focus to costing, which is an important part of management accounting. While financial accounting keeps accurate records of what has already happened, costing goes beyond that to use various forms of information to determine current and future costs as well as monitor costs that have recently been incurred.

The **sources of data** for costing will include some of the data that is also used for financial accounting, but will also extend to a range of other sources that will help to provide useful information.

Costs can therefore be seen as being:

- from the past – these are known as **historic costs**
- relating to the present – these are known as **current costs**
- projections for the future – these are known as **future costs**

We will now explain these in more detail.

financial accounting data – historic costs

The majority of financial accounting data has come from items entered in the bookkeeping ledgers, such as the following:

- invoices for sales and purchases
- payments
- receipts
- payroll

This provides an accurate record of what has already happened **in the past**. By examining the financial accounting records, a business could find out, for example:

- how much was paid in rent last year
- what was the cost of paying wages last month
- how much was paid for materials in the last quarter

By looking beyond the ledger entries to the actual invoices and other financial accounting source documents, a business could also find out in more detail, for example:

- how much the monthly rent was during each month of last year
- how many employees there were last month and how much each grade of labour was paid

■ how much was charged by suppliers for specific materials, and what quantities were bought

At this level of detail the information is more useful for costing purposes, and we can see how it can be used to build up historic cost figures.

costing data – current and future costs

While financial accounting information, and the source documents of invoices and payroll, provide accurate information about the **past** (including the recent past), we need to look at other sources so that we can calculate costs for the **current period** (the present time) and **future periods**. Not all the sources of data can be totally accurate, and businesses have to rely on estimates for some figures.

If a business needs to find the cost of materials or expenses, there may be:

■ purchase orders (for goods or services ordered already) or

■ quotations (for those that may be ordered later)

If the business wants to cost items further for the future, it may be necessary to approach possible suppliers for an estimate.

Where labour costs are concerned a business should be able to find out the current rates of pay and allow for any expected pay rises. If it is planning a new product, it should work out how long it will take to make that product. A business may have already prepared **financial forecasts (budgets)** in the past. These can provide a useful source of data for costs and income.

In Chapter 6 we will look in more detail at how we can provide information to managers based on data from various sources.

We will now use a short Case Study to help identify suitable sources of data for costing.

Case Study

ALLCOST LIMITED:
SOURCES OF DATA FOR COSTING

situation

You are employed by Allcost Limited, a manufacturer of clothes for the fashion market. A trainee in the costing department has made the following suggestions. To help him with his training you have been asked to identify which statements are correct.

1   Forecasts (budgets) will always provide a good source of data for historic costs.

2   When costing a future product the labour cost may need to be estimated by using planned labour rates and expected times to make the product.

3   Forecasts (budgets) can provide a good source of data for future costs.

4   A good source of data for historic costs are the financial accounting records and the documents that back up these records.

5   If you have a firm quotation from a supplier, this is a good source of data for current costs.

6   The number of units that are planned for is not relevant for costing purposes.

7   Payroll records which show how much people were paid and how long jobs took are useful sources of data for historic costs.

8   The prices that the business plans to charge for its products are good sources of data for estimating future income.

9   Agreements from suppliers about future prices will be used to help calculate future costs.

10   Financial accounts provide the best source of data for future costs.

r e q u i r e d

You are to

(a)   identify and list the statements that are correct

(b)   point out and comment on the statements that are incorrect

s o l u t i o n

The following statements are **correct:**

2   When costing a future product the labour cost may need to be estimated by using planned labour rates and expected times to make the product.

3   Forecasts (budgets) can provide a good source of data for future costs.

4   A good source of data for historic costs are the financial accounting records and the documents that back up these records.

5   If you have a firm quotation from a supplier, this is a good source of data for current costs.

7   Payroll records which show how much people were paid and how long jobs took are useful sources of data for historic costs.

8   The prices that the business plans to charge for its products are good sources of data for estimating future income.

9   Agreements from suppliers about future prices will be used to help calculate future costs.

The following statements are **incorrect**:

1   Forecasts (budgets) will always provide a good source of data for historic costs.

Comment: forecasts (budgets) are produced from historic costs and other data but are intended to plan for the future.

6   The number of units that are planned for is not relevant for costing purposes.

Comment: costing is often based on the number of units produced.

10   Financial accounts provide the best source of data for future costs.

Comment: financial accounts primarily provide data for financial accounting.

INTRODUCTION TO CLASSIFYING COSTS AND INCOME

Every part of an organisation incurs costs (eg administration costs and production costs) and some will generate income (eg from sales of products or services). The costing system will be able to supply management information about costs and income for each part of an organisation.

In this next section we will consider the main types of costs and income and then explain how they are analysed in relation to the different functions of the business or organisation.

the elements of cost

All businesses and organisations, whether they manufacture products or provide services, incur costs – these can be broken down into three **elements of cost**:

- materials
- labour
- expenses (overheads)

materials

- raw materials and components bought for use by a manufacturing business
- products bought for resale by a shop or a wholesaler
- service items or consumables, such as stationery, bought for use within a business or organisation

Materials range from sheet metal and plastics used in a car factory, computer chips and other components bought in by a computer manufacturer, tins of baked beans and other goods bought in by a supermarket, through to photocopying paper used in a college. Virtually all businesses and organisations incur materials costs. We will examine material costs in more detail in Chapter 4.

Labour refers to the payroll costs of all employees of the business or organisation. These costs include:

- wages paid to those who work on the production line of a manufacturing business
- wages and salaries paid to those who work for a manufacturing business but are not directly involved in the production line, eg supervisors, maintenance staff, office staff, sales people
- wages and salaries of those who work in the service industry, eg shop workers, bank employees, restaurant staff, accountants
- public sector wages, eg of central and local government employees

We will examine labour costs in more detail in Chapter 5.

Expenses is a term that refers to all other running costs of the business or organisation that cannot be included under the headings of materials and labour. Examples include rent, rates, heating, lighting, telephone, advertising, insurance, and so on.

The vast majority of expenses are also classified as **overheads** (see the next section).

income

The main source of income for the private sector is from the sale of products or services. There may also be other, smaller amounts of income, eg interest received on bank balances, rental income if a part of the premises is let to a tenant, government grants and allowances for setting up a new business or buying new technology.

When we look at coding systems in the next chapter we will see how these elements of cost are used to record costs in a costing system.

CLASSIFICATION OF COSTS BY FUNCTION AND NATURE

As well as dividing costs into materials, labour and expenses, it is also useful to show **why the costs have been incurred** – what the costs help to achieve in the organisation.

This breakdown of costs is sometimes called '**functional**' as it links to the different sections (called '**functions**') of an organisation.

We will start by showing how this classification of costs works for a manufacturing organisation. Here the two main functions are generally carried out in:

- the factory – where goods are actually produced, and

- the warehouse and offices – where the support **functions** take place (eg administration, selling and distribution, and finance)

costs in the factory – production costs

The costs incurred in the factory are **production** costs. 'Production' is the **function** into which these costs are classified.

We can divide these production costs further, into:

- **direct** costs, and

- **indirect** costs (often called overheads)

This analysis is sometimes called **classification by nature**.

Direct costs are costs that can be identified directly with each unit of output.

Indirect costs cannot be identified directly with specific units of output.

The term 'unit of output' refers to products that a manufacturer makes or services that are provided by a service organisation.

In the following explanations we will use the example of a furniture manufacturer to illustrate what we mean. For a furniture manufacturer the units of output are the chairs and other items of furniture that are manufactured.

Remember that we also divide costs into materials, labour and expenses, so that we now have up to six types of production cost:

direct costs

- **direct materials** – the cost of the materials used to make the items produced – for example the cost of the wood used to make chairs in a furniture factory

- **direct labour** – the cost of paying the employees who carry out the production – for example the cost of paying the wages of workers making chairs in a furniture factory

- **direct expense**s – there are very few examples of direct expenses, so at this stage in your studies you can normally ignore this category of cost

The total of direct costs is also called the **prime cost.**

indirect production costs (production overheads)

- **indirect materials** – the cost of materials that cannot be directly linked to specific items produced – for example the cost of replacement saw blades used in the factory making furniture

- **indirect labour** – the cost of employing people in the factory who do not actually make the products – for example the cleaners and supervisors in a furniture factory

- **indirect expenses** – the other costs of running a factory – for example the costs of heating and lighting a furniture factory

The total of direct costs and indirect production costs is simply known as **total production costs**.

costs outside the factory – non-production costs

As well as costs relating to the factory (the production costs) that we have just discussed, there are also the costs that relate to the support functions that generally take place in the warehouse or offices. These are **non-production costs** and will always be indirect costs (**overheads**). These costs are still divided into materials, labour and expenses, just like other costs.

The non-production costs may be divided into the functions of:

- administration
- selling and distribution
- finance

classification of costs – a summary

Classification of costs can be confusing, so the following may be useful to help you remember the ways that we often classify costs.

Classification by **element**:

- materials
- labour
- expenses

Classification by **function**:

- production
- administration
- selling and distribution
- finance

Classification by **nature**:

- direct costs
- indirect costs

The diagram below combines these classifications of cost and gives some examples – again based on a furniture manufacturer.

	Production ('factory') costs		Non-production ('warehouse & office') costs		
	Production *Direct Costs* *(total =* ***prime cost*** *)*	**Production** *Indirect Costs* *(overheads)*	**Administration** *Indirect* *(overheads)*	**Selling and** **Distribution** *Indirect Costs* *(overheads)*	**Finance** *Indirect Costs* *(overheads)*
Materials	Wood to make tables	Oil for production machinery	Stationery	Packing materials	
Labour	Assembly workers' wages	Production supervisors' wages	Administration staff wages	Sales peoples' wages	
Expenses	–	Factory Rent	Office Rent	Advertising costs	Interest charges on loans
	Total Production Costs		**Total Non-production Costs**		
	Total Costs				

Classification of Costs

When you have studied the diagram on the previous page, see how its principles are put into action in the Case Study which follows.

SPORTCLASS LIMITED:

CLASSIFYING COSTS FOR A MANUFACTURER

situation

You work for Sportclass Limited, a company that manufactures a range of sports equipment. The following list of costs has been compiled from the company records.

You have been asked to classify these costs in a table to illustrate to a new trainee how the company costing system works.

list of costs:

Factory insurance

Wages of employee who strings tennis racquets

Wood used to make cricket bats

Advertising costs

Wages of employee who maintains production machines in the factory

Bank overdraft interest

Cost of telephone calls in administration department

Wages of delivery driver

Floor cleaning fluid for use in the factory

Wages of office worker in administration department

Stationery used in administration office

Fuel for delivery van

solution

The table on the next page shows these costs inserted in the appropriate place according to the classification of the relevant cost.

	Production ('factory') costs		Non-production ('warehouse & office') costs		
	Production *Direct Costs*	**Production** *Indirect Costs*	**Administration** *Indirect Costs*	**Selling and Distribution** *Indirect Costs*	**Finance** *Indirect Costs*
Materials	Wood used to make cricket bats	Floor cleaning fluid for use in the factory	Stationery used in administration office	Fuel for delivery van	–
Labour	Wages of employee who strings tennis racquets	Wages of employee who maintains production machines in the factory	Wages of office worker in administration department	Wages of delivery driver	–
Expenses	–	Factory insurance	Cost of telephone calls in administration department	Advertising costs	Bank overdraft interest

COSTS IN SERVICES ORGANISATIONS

So far we have used the manufacturing industry to illustrate the way that costs can be classified by element (materials, labour and expenses) and by function (production and non-production). The same principles apply to the classification of costs in non-manufacturing organisations – businesses that provide services, for example – although the classification by function will not include 'production' in these circumstances.

Some of the costs in non-manufacturing organisations can be identified directly with the units of output, so the analysis into **direct** and **indirect costs** is still valid. For example, a bus company's units of output are passenger journeys, so direct costs would include fuel for the vehicles and the wages of the bus driver, while indirect costs would include maintaining and cleaning the buses.

The tables on the next page show how costs could be classified in a variety of non-manufacturing organisations, both into direct and indirect costs, and also into materials, labour and expenses.

The non-manufacturing organisations shown below are a hairdresser, an airline, a refuse collection company and a theme park. **Classification** in the first table is by **element** (materials, labour, expenses) and in the second by **nature** (direct and indirect costs).

Classification by element

ORGANISATION	COST	Materials	Labour	Expenses
hairdresser	Shampoo	✓		
	Stylists' wages		✓	
	Receptionists' wages		✓	
	Electricity			✓
airline	Aircraft fuel	✓		
	Pilots' wages		✓	
	Airport landing fees			✓
	Advertising			✓
refuse collection	Fuel for vehicles	✓		
	Supervisors' wages		✓	
	Operatives' wages		✓	
	Insurance			✓
theme park	Insurance			✓
	Ride staff wages		✓	
	Power for rides			✓
	Cleaning staff wages		✓	

Classification by nature

ORGANISATION	COST	Direct	Indirect
hairdresser	Shampoo	✓	
	Stylists' wages	✓	
	Receptionists' wages		✓
	Electricity		✓
airline	Aircraft fuel	✓	
	Pilots' wages	✓	
	Airport landing fees	✓	
	Advertising		✓
refuse collection	Fuel for vehicles	✓	
	Supervisors' wages		✓
	Operatives' wages	✓	
	Insurance		✓
theme park	Insurance		✓
	Ride staff wages	✓	
	Power for rides	✓	
	Cleaning staff wages		✓

The next Case Study is based on a restaurant and will help you to practise classifying costs into direct and indirect as well as by element.

ALBION RESTAURANT:
COST CLASSIFICATION

situation

Albion Restaurant is a large restaurant. Some of the costs incurred by Albion Restaurant are as follows:

(a)   wages of the cleaner

(b)   cost of heating the restaurant

(c)   wages of the chefs

(d)   telephone charges

(e)   paper table covers and napkins

(f)   cost of ingredients for meals

(g)   cleaning materials

(h)   advertising costs

(i)   maintenance contract for ovens

(j)   wages of waiters and waitresses

required

You are an accounts assistant at Albion Restaurant. You are required to classify the above costs into the six categories shown in the table below. Give your answer by entering the costs into the table.

	Direct costs	Indirect costs
Materials		
Labour		
Expenses		

solution

You classify the costs as follows:

	Direct costs	Indirect costs
Materials	(f) cost of ingredients for meals	(e) paper table covers and napkins (g) cleaning materials
Labour	(c) wages of the chefs (j) wages of waiters and waitresses*	(a) wages of the cleaner
Expenses		(b) cost of heating the restaurant (d) telephone charges (h) advertising costs (i) maintenance contract for ovens

*Note: you may have classified (j) 'wages of waiters and waitresses' as 'indirect wages'. This is an equally valid answer. A cost accounting system is designed to suit a particular organisation. There are some costs that may be treated as either direct or indirect costs, depending on the particular situation and the information required from the system. Costs which could be linked directly to cost units may be treated as overheads if this is easier and saves time without losing any useful information. Whichever treatment is used, it is important to be consistent so that, next time the cost is incurred, it is dealt with in the same way.

an alternative classification

Since expenses are usually also classified as overheads (indirect costs) you could alternatively be asked to analyse costs into 'materials, labour, and overheads'. In this type of task you should assume that 'overheads' excludes materials and labour costs. An example of this is Activity 1.6 on page 22.

the next step – coding

Once costs and income have been classified we need to use a convenient method of keeping all the data together in a logical system. One way that is often used is a **coding system**, and in the next chapter we will examine how such systems can work.

Chapter Summary

■ Costing provides information on the costs that arise from an organisation's products or services. Costing can help managers with decision making, planning and control.

■ A costing system will be designed with the needs of the organisation in mind. There is no 'one size fits all' approach, so the system can be as simple or as complex as the managers require.

■ Costing is part of the area of accounting called 'management accounting'. It concentrates on providing internal information about the future in a form that is useful and has no externally set rules that must be followed.

■ There is a variety of sources of data within the organisation for costing, as well as some useful external sources. The data used will depend on whether the information required is for historic, current or future periods.

■ Costs can be classified into the elements of materials, labour and expenses, and also by nature into direct costs and indirect costs (overheads). There are also functional classifications, the most common being production, administration, selling and distribution, and finance.

Key Terms	costing system	the system that an organisation has developed to collect information about costs so that it can be used to help with decision making, planning and control
	management accounting	the area of accounting that includes costing: it concentrates on providing internal information about the future in a form that is useful; it has no externally set rules that must be followed
	financial accounting	the area of accounting that includes book-keeping; it concentrates on providing historic information that can be used internally and also provided to external parties
	budget	a future plan for an organisation, showing all the detail in financial terms; it is usually made up of various individual budgets
	cost classification by element	grouping costs together according to the type of cost based on three categories – materials, labour and expenses (overheads)
	cost classification by nature	grouping costs together according to whether they are direct costs or indirect costs
	direct costs	costs that are directly identified with the units of output (the products or services that the organisation makes or provides)
	prime cost	a term relating to the total of direct costs; it is often used to describe the total direct cost for a unit of output
	indirect costs (overheads)	costs that are not directly identified with the units of output; these costs are divided into production and non-production costs in a manufacturing organisation
	cost of production	a term relating to the total of direct production costs and indirect production costs (production overheads)

Activities

1.1 Which **one** of the following statements is true?

(a) Financial accounting includes costing; management accounting includes bookkeeping

(b) Costing includes management accounting; bookkeeping includes financial accounting

(c) Management accounting includes financial accounting; costing includes bookkeeping

(d) Financial accounting includes bookkeeping; management accounting includes costing

Answer (a) or (b) or (c) or (d)

1.2 Which **one** of the following is a characteristic of financial accounting?

(a) Its purpose is to provide information for managers

(b) It is based on future events

(c) Its purpose is to provide information for owners and investors

(d) The timing and content of its reports is decided by managers

Answer (a) or (b) or (c) or (d)

1.3 Which **one** of the following is a characteristic of management accounting?

(a) It is based on future events

(b) It provides information for people outside the business

(c) It is based on past events

(d) It complies with company law and accounting rules

Answer (a) or (b) or (c) or (d)

1.4 Identify the following statements as being true or false by putting a tick in the relevant column of the table below.

	True	False
Management accounting must comply with company law		
Financial accounting provides information for owners and investors		
Management accounting is based on future events		
Financial accounting only provides information about what may happen in the future		

1.5   From the following table indicate two characteristics of financial accounting and two characteristics of management accounting by putting a tick in the relevant column.

Characteristic	Financial accounting	Management accounting
It is based on future events		
Its purpose is to provide information for managers		
It complies with accounting rules		
It is based on past events		

1.6   Severn Manufacturing Limited makes chairs for school and college use. The chairs have plastic seats, and tubular steel legs. You are to classify the following costs by putting a tick in the relevant column of the table below.

Cost	Materials	Labour	Overheads
Tubular steel			
Wages of employee operating the moulding machine which produces the chair seats			
Rates of factory			
Travel expenses of sales staff			
Plastic for making chair seats			
Factory heating and lighting			

1.7   Crusty Limited is in business as a bakers.

Classify the following costs by nature (direct or indirect) by putting a tick in the relevant column of the table below.

Cost	Direct	Indirect
Flour used to bake bread		
Rent of bakery		
Wages of bakers		
Repairs to baking machinery		
Currants used in buns		
Wages of bakery cleaner		
Insurance of bakery		
Salary of production manager		

1.8   Wyvern Water Limited bottles natural spring water at its plant at Walcoll at the base of the Wyvern Hills.

You are working in the costing section of Wyvern Water and are asked to classify the following costs by function (production, administration, or selling and distribution) by putting a tick in the relevant column of the table below.

Cost	Production	Administration	Selling and distribution
Wages of employees working on the bottling line			
Insurance of delivery lorries			
Cost of bottles			
Safety goggles for bottling line employees			
Advertisement for new employees			
Depreciation of bottling machinery			
Depreciation of sales staff's cars			
Attendance at a trade exhibition			
Office heating and lighting			
Sales staff salaries			

1.9   First Office Ltd manufactures a range of office furniture. The following list of costs has been compiled from the company records. You have been asked to classify these costs into a table to illustrate to a new trainee how the company costing system works.

List of costs

1.   factory rent

2.   wages of employee who makes desk legs

3.   steel used to make desk legs

4.   costs of sending out advertising brochure

5.   wages of employee who maintains production machines in the factory

6.   bank loan interest

7.   cost of photocopier maintenance contract in administration department

8.   wages of fork lift truck driver in warehouse

9.   machinery oil for use in the factory

10.   wages of accounts assistant in administration department

11.   stationery used in payroll office (part of administration)

12.   fuel for fork lift truck in warehouse

Required

Complete the table shown below by inserting the number of each of the costs on the list in the appropriate column.

	Production ('factory') costs		Non-production ('warehouse & office') costs		
	Direct costs	Indirect costs	Administration Indirect costs	Selling and Distribution Indirect costs	Finance Indirect costs
Materials					
Labour					
Expenses					

1.10 You are employed by Allsauce Limited, a manufacturer of table sauces.

A trainee in the costing department has made the following statements.

To help him with his training you have been asked to identify which of the following statements are true and which are false by putting a tick in the relevant column of the table below.

	True	False
Budgets can never be used as a source of data for historic costs		
Information to help with future costs can come from inside and outside the organisation		
Future costs are impossible to estimate		
Financial accounting records and the documents that back up these records are a good source of data for historic costs		
If you have a firm quotation from a supplier, this is a good source of data for current costs		
The number of products that the business forecasts to sell is a good source of data for estimating future income		
Costing can only be used for manufacturing businesses, not the service industry		
Financial accounts can provide a reliable source of data for future costs		
When costing a future product, the labour cost may need to be estimated by using planned labour rates and expected times to make the product		
The production level that is planned for is not relevant for costing purposes		

2 Cost centres and overhead absorption

this chapter covers...

In this chapter we look in more detail at how the basic principles of costing that we explained in the last chapter are used in a costing system.

We will start by describing 'cost centres'. These are sections of the organisation that costs can be charged to and we will use the idea of 'functional' analysis (ie different areas of the organisation) that we examined in Chapter 1.

We will also examine 'revenue centres', 'profit centres' and 'investment centres', and see how they differ from 'cost centres'.

Next we will introduce the idea of coding systems by first identifying the three main types of coding that are used in costing. We will then use the various forms of classification of costs that we have already studied to see how costs could be analysed and coded to help with costing.

In the remainder of this chapter we examine how indirect costs (overheads) can be 'absorbed' into the costs of products or services. There are three main methods for carrying this out: per unit of output, per direct labour hour, and per machine hour. Each of these methods is explained and example calculations used to demonstrate the process.

COST CENTRES

In Chapter 1 we saw that costs can be analysed by function into the main operational areas of an organisation, eg the functions of production, administration, selling and distribution, and finance. Cost centres are used to help with this functional analysis of costs.

Cost centres are sections of an organisation to which costs can be charged.

Cost centres may be based on the same functions that we have already described, or very often are based on dividing those functions up in a way that is more useful for the organisation. Thus a cost centre can be any function or section of the organisation. In a **manufacturing** business it can be an entire factory, a department of a factory, or a particular stage in the production process.

In a **service** industry it can be a shop, or group of shops in an area, a teaching department or a resources centre within a college, or a ward or operating theatre in a hospital. Any section of a business can be a cost centre – based on what is most useful for the organisation's costing system. A manager or supervisor will be responsible for each cost centre and it is this person who will be taking data from the accounts system.

analysis of costs to different cost centres

When the cost centres have been established it is necessary to ensure that the accounts system is able to provide information to the manager of each cost centre. In order to do this, separate accounts are established for each cost centre to cover the main cost headings. For example, labour costs can be split between 'wages and salaries: production', 'wages and salaries: administration', 'wages and salaries: selling and distribution', and so on.

By analysing costs in this way the accounts system is able to provide the cost centre manager with information about how much has been spent by, or charged to, the centre over the last month, quarter, half-year, or year. This information will help the manager to:

- **plan for the future**, eg by using actual costs, he/she will be able to forecast next year's costs

- **make decisions**, eg by comparing the costs of different products or services, eg whether to increase or decrease output

- **control costs**, eg by comparing actual costs with budgeted costs (see Chapter 6), he/she will be able to take steps to reduce costs

In this way the accounts system is able to tell the manager what has happened in each functional area in terms of financial information.

where does the information come from?

The sources of information for the analysis of costs include:

- purchase orders and purchase invoices, for materials and expenses costs
- payroll schedules, for labour costs
- bills and cash receipts, for expenses costs

The amounts of each cost are then analysed to the cost centre which has incurred the cost. The diagram below shows how this process works. A firm's policy manual should give details of which costs are to be charged to which cost centre.

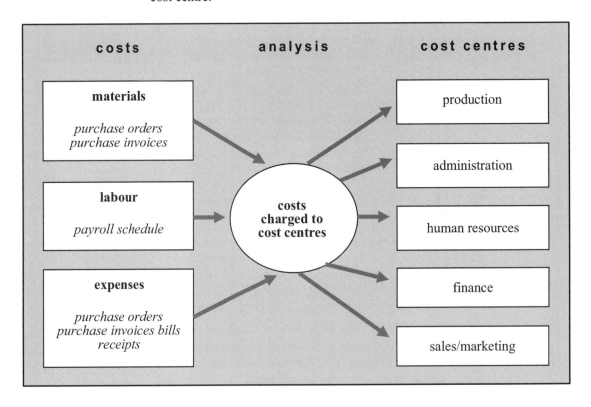

REVENUE CENTRES

Some organisations use revenue centres as responsibility centres where managers are responsible for generating sales revenue. Unlike cost centres (and profit centres which we will consider next), revenue centres do not incorporate costs, but are only concerned with revenue.

Revenue centres are sections of a business to which income can be identified.

Revenue centres could be used (for example) where sales teams are organised into regions, and each sales region could then be a revenue centre. Each regional sales manager would then be accountable for the sales generated in their region.

PROFIT CENTRES

For some sections of businesses the cost centre approach of analysing costs is taken to a further level by also analysing sales income to centres. As sales income less costs equals profit, such centres are called profit centres. Note that the source of information on sales comes from sales orders and sales invoices.

Profit centres are sections of a business to which costs can be charged, income can be identified, and profit can be calculated.

From the definition we can see that profit centres have both costs and income. It follows, therefore, that profit centres will be based on sections of the business that make products or services (incur costs) and sell them to customers (receive income from sales). For example, a clothing manufacturer might have 'dresses' as a profit centre, as shown in the following diagram:

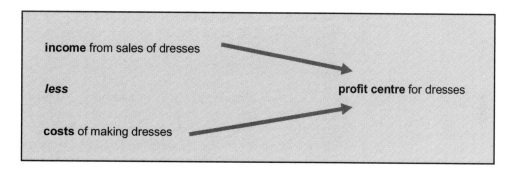

Note that many cost centres provide support services within a business or organisation, so cannot become profit centres because they do not have any significant income. For example, the administration department of a business is a cost centre to which costs can be charged, but it does not receive any income. As we have seen, profit centres both incur costs and generate income.

Managers of profit centres will be getting information from the accounting system about the costs incurred and the income generated by their centre. By deducting costs from income, they can calculate the profit made and can make comparisons with previous periods (eg last month, last quarter, last year, etc) and also with other profit centres (eg 'our profit was higher than yours last month').

INVESTMENT CENTRES

Investment centres are sections of the organisation where not only can information on income and costs be gathered, but also information on the amount of investment. Investment could take the form of non-current (fixed) assets (for example, buildings or machinery), as well as inventory and other current assets.

In this way the performance of the investment centre can be measured not just by the level of profit (as in a profit centre), but also by comparing the profit with the amount invested in that part of the business. An investment centre can therefore be like a mini business within the main business. An example of an investment centre could be an individual shop within a chain of shops operated by the same company.

The term 'responsibility centre' is sometimes used to describe cost centres, profit centres, and investment centres.

CODING SYSTEMS

Coding systems are used to organise and analyse data. Coding systems are used extensively in costing, and are also used in many other situations. There are three main types of coding system that we must be able to identify and explain.

■ **Numeric coding**

Here, each code is made up entirely of **numbers**. It is used extensively in accounting and costing for account numbers and identification codes, and also used for everyday applications, eg phone numbers and PIN numbers. If all the available numbers are used, there will be a large number of codes available – for a two digit code there are $10 \times 10 = 100$ unique codes. A drawback of this system is that a numeric code may easily be forgotten.

■ **Alphabetic coding**

Each alphabetic code is made up entirely of **letters**. Many website addresses are really alphabetic codes, eg www.osbornebooks.co.uk. An alphabetic code has the advantage of being easier to remember than numbers if the 'words' created make sense, and can also provide many more available codes than numeric ones. For example, even for two letter codes from aa to zz there are $26 \times 26 = 676$ unique codes.

■ **Alpha-numeric coding**

This type of code is made up of both **letters and numbers in any combination**. A UK postcode is an example of alpha-numeric coding. Here the first two letters represent the main location (eg WR for Worcester) which helps the user. Some accounting systems use alpha-numeric coding for customer accounts, for example A01 to A99 for customers whose names begin with A, or CAM001 for a customer whose name begins with 'CAM', eg Cameron, Campion, Camus. These, like postcodes, are relatively easy to remember.

USE OF CODING IN COSTING

Codes in a costing system are used to collect data about costs and income and analyse these amounts into categories that the organisation finds useful. Sales and purchase invoices and other documents that contain data to be analysed will be 'coded'. The value amount together with the code will be entered into a computerised costing system or database.

We have learned about classifying costs:

■ by element (materials, labour, expenses)

■ by nature (direct and indirect)

We have also learned that cost centres, revenue centres, profit centres and investment centres can be used to identify sections of a business. A coding system can use these ways of classifying costs and classifying income.

For example, a clothing manufacturer might use a coding system where the first part of the code denotes the profit centre or cost centre, and the second part of the code (the sub-code) denotes a sub-classification based on whether the data is sales income, direct cost, or indirect cost.

If this code system was **alpha-numeric**, the amount of income from the **sales of dresses** could be coded to:

> B10   if B related to the profit centre 'dresses'
>
>   and 10 was the sub-code for 'sales income'

The cost of machinists' **wages in the sewing section** could be coded to:

> H30   if H related to the cost centre 'sewing section'
>
>   and 30 was the sub-code for 'direct cost'

Remember that the coding system will be designed to suit the needs of each individual organisation. The above example is quite a simple one, but demonstrates how a coding system could work.

We will now use a Case Study to illustrate in more detail how a coding system works.

CLASSY LIMITED: USING COSTING CODES

situation

Classy Limited is an educational company that runs courses for accountancy trainees and other office staff.

It uses a coding system for the elements of cost (materials, labour and expenses), with further classification into direct and indirect costs.

The coding used is as follows:

Element	Code	Nature	Code
Materials	100	Direct	X
		Indirect	Y
Labour	200	Direct	X
		Indirect	Y
Expenses	300	Direct	X
		Indirect	Y

required

Identify codes for the following costs:

- wages of tutor
- rent of classroom
- handouts and stationery for students' use
- power, light and heat in classroom
- wages of manager
- insurance of equipment

solution

• wages of tutor	200X
• rent of classroom	300Y
• handouts and stationery for students' use	100X
• power, light and heat in classroom	300Y
• wages of manager	200Y
• insurance of equipment	300Y

Note: for an example of an alternative coding system, see Activity 2.3 on page 44.

ABSORPTION OF OVERHEADS

We saw in Chapter 1 that costs can be analysed by nature into:

■ Direct Costs – those that can be identified directly with each unit of output, and

■ Indirect Costs (overheads) – those that cannot be identified directly with specific units of output.

When we are calculating the cost of a unit of output (for example a chair made by a furniture manufacturer) the direct costs will be straightforward to calculate. For example, the direct costs of a chair could be made up of:

Direct materials (wood)	£15.00
Direct labour (wages of carpenter: 2 hours at £12 per hour)	£24.00
	———
Total direct costs	£39.00

The indirect costs cannot be directly identified with specific units of output (in this case individual chairs), so a suitable method of spreading these overhead costs over all the units of output must be used.

All the overhead absorption methods that we can use are based on sharing overhead costs that have first been collected in suitable responsibility centres (cost centres, profit centres or investment centres). We will mainly be using examples where a business has just one manufacturing cost centre, and all the factory overhead costs are collected there. Note that in a manufacturing environment the only overhead costs that are absorbed into the units of output are production overheads – the indirect costs that are incurred in the factory. The non-production costs (typically administration, selling and distribution and finance) are not absorbed, but are normally accounted for separately.

There are three absorption methods that we need to understand and be able to use in calculations. Each method determines an 'overhead absorption rate' (sometimes abbreviated to 'OAR') based on budgeted costs and budgeted output that is then applied to each unit of product (or service). The choice of method used is sometimes known as the absorption base.

units of output method

This is the simplest method and is only suitable for organisations where all the units of output are identical (or very similar). The budgeted manufacturing overheads are simply divided by the budgeted number of units (the output) to produce a figure that can easily be used to represent the indirect cost part of the unit cost.

worked example

A furniture manufacturer only makes chairs. The budgeted overhead costs in the only production cost centre are £85,000 for the year. The budgeted number of chairs to be made in a year is 1,700.

The overhead absorption rate per chair will be:

$$\frac{\text{Budgeted overheads}}{\text{Budgeted units of output}} \quad \frac{£85,000}{1,700 \text{ chairs}} = £50 \text{ per chair}$$

Using the previous data, the total cost per chair would then be:

Direct materials (wood)	£15.00
Direct labour (wages of carpenter: 2 hours at £12 per hour)	£24.00
Total direct costs	£39.00
Overheads absorbed	£50.00
Total cost per chair	£89.00

This method would not be appropriate if the organisation made different products (for example chairs and tables). This is because items that take longer and are more expensive to make should logically bear more overheads than items that are cheaper and quicker to manufacture. The units of output method would not do this and would simply absorb exactly the same amount of overhead onto each item made – whatever it was.

direct labour hours method

This method absorbs overheads onto the products in proportion to the number of direct labour hours that each type of product should take to manufacture. In this way it can cope with organisations that make different products, since the products that take most labour time to manufacture will incur more overheads than those that are quicker and cheaper to make.

This method calculates an overhead absorption rate based on each budgeted direct labour hour that will be worked. This rate is then applied to each type of product based on how many labour hours should be taken to make one unit of that product.

The calculation of the overhead absorption rate per direct labour hour is:

$$\frac{\text{Budgeted overheads}}{\text{Budgeted direct labour hours}}$$

worked example

A furniture manufacturer makes chairs and tables. The budgeted overhead costs in the only production cost centre are £85,000 for the year. The budgeted direct labour hours to be worked in the factory in a year are 4,000 hours. Each chair takes 2 direct labour hours to make, and each table takes 5 direct labour hours.

The overhead absorption rate per direct labour hour is:

$$\frac{£85,000}{4,000 \text{ hours}} = £21.25 \text{ per direct labour hour}$$

This rate can then be applied to both chairs and tables (and any other products). If we assume that the direct costs per chair are the same as in the earlier example, the total cost per chair will be:

Direct materials (wood)	£15.00
Direct labour (wages of carpenter: 2 hours at £12 per hour)	£24.00
Total direct costs	£39.00
Overheads absorbed (2 direct labour hours at £21.25 per hour)	£42.50
Total cost per chair	£81.50

The amount of overheads that would be absorbed into the cost of a table would be 5 hours x £21.25 = £106.25.

This overhead absorption method is particularly appropriate where several different products are made and the manufacturing process is labour intensive.

machine hours method

Where a manufacturing process intensively uses expensive machinery, the machine hours method of overhead absorption will often produce fairer results than using labour hours.

The logic and method of calculation is similar to using direct labour hours, but instead the number of machine hours is used. An overhead absorption rate is calculated based on each budgeted machine hour that will be used. This rate is then applied to each type of product based on how many machine hours should be taken to make one unit of that product.

The calculation of the overhead absorption rate per machine hour is:

$$\frac{\text{Budgeted overheads}}{\text{Budgeted machine hours}}$$

worked example

A manufacturer uses an automated process to cut wood and other material to make flat-pack furniture. The cost of using the machinery is a major part of the manufacturing overheads. The budgeted overhead costs in the only production cost centre are £96,000 for the year. The budgeted machine hours to be used in the factory in a year are 3,000 hours. Two of the products made are bedside cabinets and wardrobes. Each bedside cabinet takes 30 minutes of machine time to make, and each wardrobe takes 1 hour 30 minutes of machine time.

The overhead absorption rate per machine hour is:

$$\frac{£96,000}{3,000 \text{ hours}} = £32.00 \text{ per machine hour}$$

The manufacturing overhead absorbed into each product will be:

Bedside cabinet:	30 minutes at £32.00 per hour =	£16.00
Wardrobe:	1 hour 30 minutes at £32.00 per hour =	£48.00

These amounts would then be added to the direct costs to arrive at the total cost for each of the products in the same way as in the previous examples.

rounding

In the examples that we have used so far all the figures have worked out to the pound or penny without carrying out any rounding. Sometimes this will not be the case, and you may be presented with calculations which require rounding, either in the overhead absorption rate or in the amount absorbed into each product, or both. Be careful to follow any instructions about rounding that are given. We will demonstrate this in the following Case Study.

THE COMPARISON COMPANY:
DIRECT LABOUR AND MACHINE HOURS
ABSORPTION

situation

The Comparison Company makes a range of products in its factory. The factory is a single cost centre. The manufacturing process is carried out partly using direct labour and partly using machinery. The Finance Director is keen to see how using machine hours as a basis for overhead absorption would compare with the existing direct labour hours basis. The following data is available:

Budgeted factory data:

Annual production overheads	£249,500
Annual direct labour hours	8,400 hours
Annual machine hours	5,250 hours

	Product A	Product B
Direct costs per unit:		
Direct materials	£55.30	£19.50
Direct labour at £14.00 per hour	£42.00	£14.00
Total	£97.30	£33.50
Machine time per unit	2 hours	35 minutes

required

Calculate the overhead absorption rates (OARs) using the alternative absorption bases of direct labour hours and machine hours. Calculate the hourly rates to 4 decimal places of £.

Use each of the absorption bases to calculate alternative total costs for one unit each of product A and product B to the nearest penny.

solution

Overhead absorption rates:

Direct labour hour method:	£249,500 / 8,400 hours	= £29.7024 per hour
Machine hour method:	£249,500 / 5,250 hours	= £47.5238 per hour

Total product costs:

	Using Direct Labour Hours		Using Machine Hours	
	Product A	**Product B**	**Product A**	**Product B**
	£	£	£	£
Direct costs:				
Direct materials	55.30	19.50	55.30	19.50
Direct labour	42.00	14.00	42.00	14.00
	97.30	33.50	97.30	33.50
Overheads (see calculation below)	89.11	29.70	95.05	27.72
Total cost	186.41	63.20	192.35	61.22

Calculation of overheads absorbed (all rounded to nearest penny)

Using Direct Labour Hours:

    Product A   3 hours* x £29.7024   = £89.11

    Product B   1 hour* x £29.7024   = £29.70

*Number of hours calculated from hourly rate of £14.00 given in data.

Using Machine Hours:

    Product A   2 hours x £47.5238   = £95.05

    Product B   35 minutes x £47.5238 / 60 = £27.72

absorption with more than one cost centre

So far we have examined the situation where there is only one cost centre in a factory. Sometimes more than one manufacturing cost centre is used by an organisation and costs and other data are collected in each cost centre. In these situations the products will often travel through the cost centres as they are being made, and we need to reflect this in the way that overheads are absorbed.

Each manufacturing cost centre is treated separately for overhead absorption. The budgeted data from each cost centre will be used to calculate separate overhead absorption rates for each cost centre. These rates will then be applied to the products – typically based on the time that a product is processed in each cost centre (in direct labour hours or machine hours). The total overhead absorbed into each product will therefore be made up of overheads from each relevant cost centre.

This technique is also useful for service organisations with more than one direct cost centre, and the following Case Study will illustrate this.

Case Study

THE CAR MAINTENANCE COMPANY: ABSORPTION USING TWO COST CENTRES

The Car Maintenance Company carries out vehicle servicing. The work is carried out in two cost centres:

• The general maintenance cost centre, which is labour intensive, and

• The electronic tuning cost centre, which is machine intensive.

The following budgeted data relates to a year:

	General Maintenance	Electronic Tuning
Cost centre overheads	£119,000	£83,000
Direct Labour Hours	6,200	
Machine Hours		2,080

One of the types of service that the company offers is a 'Major Service'. This involves the following direct costs:

• Parts costing £48.00

• 4 hours direct labour at £15.00 per hour

When a vehicle undergoes a major service, it takes:

• 3.5 hours direct labour in General Maintenance

• 1 hour of machine time in Electronic Tuning

required

• Calculate the overhead absorption rates for General Maintenance and Electronic Tuning, rounding each to the nearest penny.

• Calculate the total cost of carrying out a Major Service rounded to the nearest penny.

solution

The overhead absorption rates are calculated as follows:

General Maintenance:

   £119,000 / 6,200 hours = £19.19 per direct labour hour

Electronic Tuning:

   £83,000 / 2,080 hours = £39.90 per machine hour

The total cost of a Major Service is as follows:

	£
Direct Materials (parts)	48.00
Direct Labour (4 hours at £15)	60.00
Overheads:	
General Maintenance	
3.5 hours at £19.19	67.17
Electronic Tuning	
1 hour at £39.90	39.90
	———
Total cost	215.07
	———

**Chapter
Summary**

■   Cost centres are used to help with the functional analysis of costs. Costs are collected in cost centres, and can be used to provide information to the manager responsible for the performance of a specific cost centre.

■   Profit centres are used to collect data about both costs and income, and can therefore provide information about the profitability of that part of the organisation.

■   Investment centres are used to collect data about income, costs and the amount invested. In this way profitability can be compared to the level of investment.

■   Coding systems are used in many contexts and there are many examples of codes that we all use every day including postcodes and dialling codes. Different code structures have different advantages and disadvantages.

■   Coding is used extensively for analysis of costs and income in costing systems. The types used mainly in costing are numeric, alphabetic and alpha-numeric. Codes may be used to analyse costs based on element, nature, cost centre or function or a combination of these classifications.

■   Indirect costs (overheads) can be incorporated into product costs by using a method of absorption.

■   Three common methods of absorption of overheads are: units of output method, direct labour hours method, and machine hours method. All use budgeted data to calculate overhead absorption rates that can then be applied to products or services.

■   Units of output method of absorption is suitable when all units of output are identical or similar. Direct labour hours method is suitable when there is a variety of products or services and the process is labour intensive. Machine hours method is suitable for machine intensive processes and can be used where there is a variety of units of output.

<table>
<tr><td rowspan="14" style="vertical-align:top">Key Terms</td></tr>
</table>

cost centre	a section of an organisation to which costs can be charged. The number and type of cost centre would depend on the requirements of the organisation
profit centre	a section of an organisation to which costs can be charged, income can be identified, and profits can be calculated
investment centre	a section of an organisation to which costs can be charged, income can be identified and investment can be measured
coding system	a way of using unique headings to analyse data. They can also be used to place the data in logical order if required
numeric code	a code made up entirely of numbers
alphabetic code	a code made up entirely of letters of the alphabet
alpha-numeric code	a code made up of a combination of numbers and letters
absorption	means of incorporating indirect costs (overheads) into costs of units of output
absorption base	chosen method of absorption used by an organisation
overhead absorption rate (OAR)	the rate used to absorb overheads into products or services based on budgeted figures
units of output method	a method of absorption based on dividing budgeted overheads by budgeted number of units to provide an overhead absorption rate per unit
direct labour hours method	a method of absorption based on dividing budgeted overheads by budgeted direct labour hours to provide an overhead absorption rate per direct labour hour
machine hours method	a method of absorption based on dividing budgeted overheads by budgeted machine hours to provide an overhead absorption rate per machine hour

Activities

2.1 Identify which **one** of the following lists could be used as cost centres for a company that manufactures windows.

(a) Materials; Labour; Overheads

(b) Frame Construction; Glazing; Administration; Distribution

(c) Direct Costs; Indirect Costs

(d) Prime Cost; Manufacturing Overheads; Non-Production Overheads

Answer (a) or (b) or (c) or (d)

2.2 Cliff Beach Limited is a company that owns two shops in a seaside town. One shop is called Clifftop, and the other is called Beachside. Each shop is an investment centre. Administration for the shops is carried out in a separate cost centre.

The following is an extract from the coding manual used by the company.

Investment or Cost Centre	Code
Administration	A
Beachside Shop	B
Clifftop Shop	C
Revenue, Cost, or Investment	**Code**
Shop sales revenue	100
Shop purchases for resale	200
Labour costs	300
Overheads	400
Investment in shop assets	900

Each code consists of a letter followed by a 3 digit number.

Complete the following table with the appropriate codes.

Transaction Code	Code
Sales in Beachside shop	
Cost of paying wages of shop staff at Clifftop	
Purchase of new display shelving for Beachside	
Purchase of goods for resale at Clifftop shop	
Cost of electricity at Clifftop shop	
Cost of paying wages of company administrator	

2.3   Roadways Limited is a transport company that provides a delivery service for its customers' goods.

It uses a coding system based on material, labour and overheads, with further classification into direct and indirect costs.

The coding used is as follows:

	Code	Nature	Code
Materials	A	Direct	100
		Indirect	200
Labour	B	Direct	100
		Indirect	200
Overheads	C	Direct	100
		Indirect	200

Code the following costs, extracted from invoices and payroll, using the table below.

Cost	Code
Wages of drivers	
Loss in value (depreciation) of vehicles	
Fuel for vehicles	
Rent of premises	
Wages of maintenance staff	
Advanced driving courses	

2.4   Eagle Books, a publisher of textbooks and general books, uses a numerical coding structure. The business is split into four divisions: academic textbooks, novels, children's books and sports books – each division is a profit centre. There is also a cost centre for administration. Each profit/cost centre has a two-digit code; each income or cost has a three-digit code. Therefore each transaction is coded as xx/xxx.

An extract from the company's coding policy manual is as follows:

profit/cost centre code	profit/cost centre name
20	academic textbooks
30	novels
40	children's books
50	sports books
60	administration

analysis code	revenue or expense
110	printing
210	basic pay
220	overtime
230	holiday pay
310	authors' royalties
320	rates
330	heating and lighting
340	telephone
350	building maintenance
360	vehicle running costs
370	advertising
410	sales to bookshops
420	sales to wholesalers

From the coding policy manual extract given, you are to code the following income or cost transactions using the table below.

Transaction	Code
Sales invoice showing the sale of £14,750 of academic textbooks to Orton Book Wholesalers Limited	
Printer's bill of £22,740 for printing sports books	
Payroll summary showing overtime of £840 last month in the children's book section	
Payment of £1,540 for advertising sports books in the magazine 'Sport Today'	
Telephone bill of £1,200 for the administration department	
Royalties of £88,245 paid to children's book authors	
Sales invoice showing the sale of £1,890 of novels to the Airport Bookshop	

2.5 You work in the costing section of Doorcraft Ltd, a company that manufactures wooden doors. Each door is made by cutting up wood using a powered saw, and the wood pieces are screwed together. The door is then machine sanded and finally polished by hand.

An extract from the company's coding policy manual is as follows:

Each code is made up of three digits:

- the first digit shows the cost centre

- the second digit shows whether the cost is direct or indirect

- the third digit shows the element of cost (materials, labour, expenses)

Extract from cost centre list:

1   Factory – Wood cutting and door assembly

2   Factory – Door sanding and polishing

3   Office

Extract from list of analysis codes (second digit):

1   Direct

2   Indirect

Extract from list of analysis codes (third digit):

1   Material

2   Labour

3   Expenses

From the coding policy manual extract given, you are to code the following expense transactions, using the table below.

Transaction	Code
Wages of the carpenter who assembles the doors	
Sandpaper	
Saw sharpening service	
Wages of the cleaner who works in the door sanding and polishing section	
Office telephone costs	
Wood for manufacturing doors	
Wages of office worker	

2.6   A company has a single cost centre in its factory where several different products are made. The following budgeted data relates to the factory:

Overheads	£153,000
Total production (all products)	38,250
Direct labour hours	31,875
Machine hours	12,750

Product A is one of the products made in the factory. It has the following data per unit:

Direct materials cost	£11.00
Direct labour cost	£30.00
Direct labour hours	3 hours
Machine hours	2 hours

- Complete the following table to show the alternative overhead absorption rates and the total cost per unit of Product A using each absorption method.

- State which one of the three overhead absorption methods is least likely to be appropriate for this company, and why.

Overhead absorption method	Units of output £	Direct labour hours £	Machine hours £
Overhead absorption rate			
Product A costs:			
Direct materials			
Direct labour			
Overheads			
Total costs			

2.7   A company has a single cost centre in its factory where several different products are made. The following budgeted data relates to the factory:

Overheads	£243,850
Direct labour hours	71,925
Machine hours	65,750

Product Q is one of the products made in the factory. It has the following data per unit:

Direct materials cost	£21.60
Direct labour cost at £11.00 per hour	£33.00
Machine hours	2.5 hours

•   Complete the following table to show the alternative overhead absorption rates and the total cost per unit of Product Q using each absorption method. Round the overhead absorption rate to 4 decimal places of £, and calculate the overhead absorbed to the nearest penny

Overhead absorption method	Direct labour hours £	Machine hours £
Overhead absorption rate		
Product Q costs:		
Direct materials		
Direct labour		
Overheads		
Total costs		

2.8 Duo Limited is a manufacturing company with two cost centres in its factory; Fabrication and Assembly. Both cost centres are labour intensive. The following data relates to the cost centres:

	Fabrication	Assembly	Total
Budgeted indirect costs	£135,600	£101,350	£236,950
Budgeted direct labour hours	44,500	31,900	76,400

One of the products made in the factory is Product M. Its manufacture takes 4 hours direct labour in Fabrication, and 1 hour 45 minutes direct labour in Assembly.

Using the following tables, calculate the overhead absorption rates and the overheads that are absorbed into each unit of Product M. Round all amounts to the nearest penny.

	Budgeted indirect costs £	Budgeted direct labour hours	Overhead absorption rate £
Fabrication			
Assembly			

Product M	Direct labour hours per unit	Overhead absorption rate £	Overhead absorbed £
Fabrication			
Assembly			
Total			

3 Cost behaviour

this chapter covers...

The topic covered in this chapter is 'cost behaviour'. This term relates to the way that costs react to changes in output or activity levels. Some costs remain the same in total ('fixed' costs), others change directly with changes in output ('variable' costs), while others contain an element of each of these behaviours ('semi-variable' costs). Another type of cost behaviour is when total costs rise in steps when output increases – called stepped costs.

We will learn about the features of these different cost behaviours, and will be able to identify the behaviour of a variety of costs for different organisations. We will then see how this knowledge of cost behaviour can be used to help calculate total costs and unit costs in a range of situations.

COST BEHAVIOUR

So far in this book we have seen how we can classify costs according to the main **elements** of materials, labour and expenses. We can classify the **nature** of costs as direct or indirect, and also according to their **function**. We can use cost centres to help with this analysis.

One further way that costs can be classified is based on the way that costs change when the level of output changes. This is known as **cost behaviour**.

what does 'cost behaviour' mean?

What we mean by **cost behaviour** is the way in which costs alter with **changes in the level of output or activity**. For example:

- for a **manufacturing** organisation, the **quantity of items** produced
- for a **service** organisation, the **volume of services** provided

When the output of an organisation changes, some costs will stay the same, while others will change. The main ways that costs may behave are:

- **fixed** costs (including stepped costs)
- **variable** costs
- **semi-variable** costs

Remember that we are only interested here in the way that costs change because of changes in output or activity – not because of changes in price or any other reason unrelated to output or activity.

fixed costs

Fixed costs do not alter when the level of output or activity changes.

For example, the rent of a furniture factory will not change just because a different number of chairs were made in one month compared with the previous month. The factory rent is therefore said to behave as a fixed cost. This does not mean that the factory rent will never change – it means that it does not change because the output of the factory changes.

Suppose that the rent for a furniture factory was £5,000 per month. This total monthly rent would be the same whether 100 chairs were made or 1,000 chairs were made. It would still be £5,000 per month if the factory shut down for a holiday and no chairs at all were made. If we drew a graph based on the total rent and the number of chairs made, we would see that it produced a straight horizontal line, as follows:

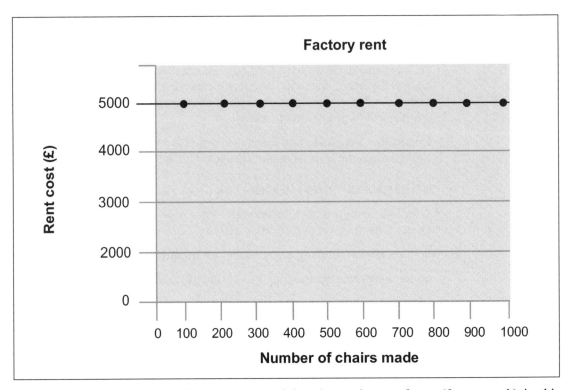

Notice that we are examining the total cost of rent (for a month) in this example, and can see that this does not change. If we were to calculate the cost of rent per chair made then we would see that the more chairs that were made, the lower the rent cost would be for each chair. This is a feature of fixed costs – the cost is fixed in total and this means that the greater the output the lower the cost per unit. Lower costs per unit are the result of spreading fixed costs over more units.

The fixed costs described above are also known as **permanent fixed costs**. This means that the costs will remain fixed throughout the expected range of activity. Another form of fixed costs is **stepped fixed costs** (or simply **stepped costs**). This occurs when a cost is fixed for a limited range of activity, but the costs then increase to a higher fixed level for activity in a higher range.

For example, suppose a furniture manufacturer hired a specialised woodworking machine to make chairs. If one machine could make up to 500 chairs per month, then a second machine would be required if output was between 500 and 1,000 chairs per month. If the cost of hiring each machine was £300 per month, then the fixed cost would step up from a level of £300 per month to a level of £600 per month if output exceeded 500 chairs per month.

variable costs

Variable costs change in proportion to the level of output or activity.

For example, if the output doubles then the total of a variable cost would also double.

The total cost of wood for chairs that are made in a furniture factory will depend on the number of chairs that are made. If more chairs are made, the total cost of wood will be greater. We would expect the cost of wood to make 200 chairs to be twice as much as the cost of wood to make 100 chairs. This is because the wood for each chair will cost the same, and more chairs means more wood. We can ignore issues like quantity discounts when considering cost behaviour at this stage of our studies.

Suppose that the cost of wood for each chair is £20. That means that if 100 chairs are made, the total cost of wood will be £20 x 100 = £2,000. If 200 chairs were made, the total cost of wood would be £20 x 200 = £4,000, and so on. A graph of the total cost of wood would look like this:

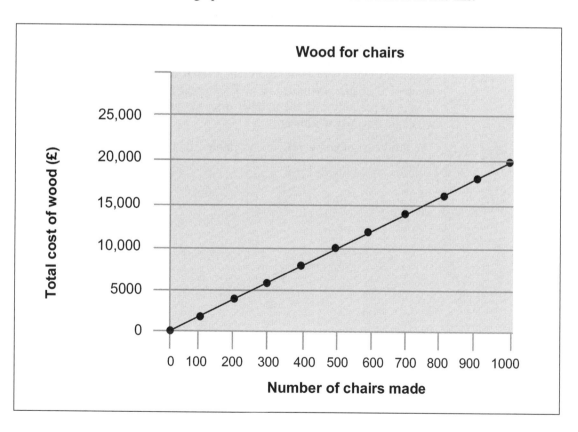

Total variable costs will always look like this on a graph. The cost line starts in the bottom left corner where there is zero output and zero cost. The points then form a straight line as the total cost rises in proportion to the output.

When the output increases, variable costs per unit do not change. In our example the cost of wood per chair remained £20 regardless of the number of chairs made. Contrast this with fixed costs that stay the same in total, but reduce as a cost per item when the output rises.

semi – variable costs

Semi-variable costs contain both a fixed element and a variable element.

When output (or activity) changes, part of the cost will remain fixed, and part of the cost will change in proportion to the activity. This means that if output doubled, a semi-variable cost would increase, but it would not double – the increase would be less than that because the fixed costs stay the same.

Suppose that in a furniture factory a person was employed as an assembler - to fit the parts of the chairs together. If the assembler was paid a basic salary of £1,000 per month, plus a bonus amount of £1 for every chair that he or she assembled, then the cost of employing this person would be a semi-variable cost. The basic pay would not change no matter how many chairs were assembled – this part would represent a **fixed cost**. The bonus based on the number of chairs assembled would represent a **variable cost** as it would change in proportion to the number of chairs assembled. Together the total would be a **semi-variable** cost.

The **total cost** of employing the assembler for a month will look like this on a graph:

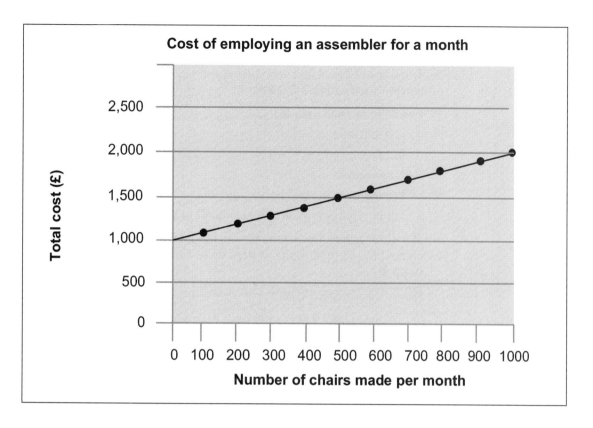

The total cost follows a straight line that starts on the far left at the axis where the only cost is the fixed cost. This is because when no chairs are made the assembler will be paid just the basic £1,000. The line then rises by £1 for each chair. In this example, the fixed element of the cost is £1,000 per month, and the variable element is £1 per chair. The graph is really like a fixed cost graph with a variable cost graph added on top of it.

Note that the total labour cost per unit for a semi-variable cost will reduce as the output increases.

IDENTIFYING COST BEHAVIOUR

As we saw in the last section the main types of cost behaviour are costs that are fixed, stepped, variable and semi-variable. It is important that you can identify how a certain cost is likely to behave if you are provided with some basic information. This is easy to do if you understand the different relationships between cost and output and think the situation through.

The following points and examples may help with identification of cost behaviour.

■ If the cost is based on a time period and the amount does not depend on output then it will be a **fixed** cost.

Examples of fixed costs are:
- rent and rates
- insurance
- staff salaries
- heating
- fall in value (known as 'depreciation') of vehicles

■ If the cost is based on a time period, but it is also subject to a maximum output level (beyond which it steps up to a higher level) then it will be a **stepped** cost.

Examples of stepped costs are:
- machinery hire that has an output limit per machine
- call centre staff salaries where additional staff are needed to deal with an increase in number of calls

■ If the cost is based on a unit of output (for example per item manufactured or per service provided) and is the same for each one, then it is a **variable** cost.

Examples of variable costs are:
- materials used in production
- labour paid per unit produced
- packaging materials
- expenses charged per unit produced (eg royalties)
- vehicle fuel for a delivery organisation

■ If the cost is based on a combination of time period cost and per unit cost then it will behave as a **semi-variable** cost.

Examples of semi-variable costs are:
- labour paid on a weekly wage basis plus a production bonus
- power for production machinery if charged at a flat rate plus a charge based on amount used

We will now use two Case Studies, each based on a different type of organisation, to practise identifying the way that costs behave.

JEAN'S JEANS:
IDENTIFYING COST BEHAVIOUR

situation

You work in the costing section of Jean's Jeans, a company that makes clothing. You have been asked to identify how each of the costs shown below is likely to behave, as a preliminary part of a cost planning exercise.

costs

- material for clothes

- factory rent

- power for sewing machines in factory (charged per unit of electricity)

- factory supervisors' wages (paid a flat rate plus a production-based bonus)

- packaging materials

- telephone (charged at a flat rate plus an amount per call; more calls are made when more clothes are being produced)

- office rates

- delivery drivers' pay (paid a flat rate plus a bonus per package delivered)

- factory heating

required

Complete the following table by inserting the costs into the most appropriate column.

Fixed costs	Variable costs	Semi-variable costs

solution

Fixed costs	Variable costs	Semi-variable costs
Factory rent	Material for clothes	Factory supervisors' wages
Office rates	Power for sewing machines in factory	Telephone
Factory heating	Packaging materials	Delivery drivers' pay

Case Study

BLOWN AWAY:
IDENTIFYING COST BEHAVIOUR

situation

You work for Blown Away, a company that provides hot air balloon rides. Each trip is for two passengers and a pilot, with a recovery vehicle following on the ground. You have been asked to identify how each of the costs shown below is likely to behave, as a preliminary part of a cost planning exercise.

costs

- insurance (charged per year, regardless of number of flights)
- fuel for balloon
- pilot's pay (a basic amount plus a bonus per flight)
- car tax (vehicle excise duty) for recovery vehicle
- pay for recovery vehicle driver (paid per flight)
- refreshments for passengers after every flight
- advertising costs
- annual rent of take-off site
- fuel for recovery vehicle
- annual subscription to weather forecasting service
- use of mobile telephone for contact between pilot and recovery vehicle driver (paid at a flat rate plus a charge per call)

required

Complete the following table by inserting the costs into the most appropriate column.

Fixed costs	Variable costs	Semi-variable costs

solution

Fixed costs	Variable costs	Semi-variable costs
Insurance	Fuel for balloon	Pilots' pay
Car tax for recovery vehicle	Pay for vehicle driver	Use of mobile telephone
Advertising costs	Refreshments for passengers	
Rent of take-off site	Fuel for recovery vehicle	
Subscription to weather forecasting service		

COST BEHAVIOUR CALCULATIONS

Now that we have studied cost behaviour and are able to identify fixed, variable, and semi-variable costs, we can use this knowledge to carry out calculations.

Study the worked example on the next page.

worked example

If we know that variable costs of a product total £15 per unit, and that fixed costs are £1,000 per month, we can calculate the total costs for a given number of units.

- 100 units made in a month would result in costs of

Variable Costs	(£15 x 100)	£1,500
Fixed Costs		£1,000
Total Costs		£2,500

- 500 units made in a month would result in costs of

Variable Costs	(£15 x 500)	£7,500
Fixed Costs		£1,000
Total Costs		£8,500

We can also calculate the total cost per unit (often known as the 'unit cost') by dividing the total costs by the number of units.

- If 100 units are made, the cost per unit would be

  £2,500 ÷ 100 = £25.00 per unit

- If 500 units are made, the cost per unit would be

  £8,500 ÷ 500 = £17.00 per unit

Notice that by making more units, the unit cost is lower. This will always occur where part of the total cost behaves as a fixed cost, since there are more units to spread the fixed cost over.

If required, the unit cost could be analysed in various ways.

Suppose that in our example the variable cost of £15 per unit is made up of materials £10, and labour £5, and the fixed cost of £1,000 per month is overheads. We could then calculate the following alternative costs, based on producing 100 or 500 units per month.

	100 units per month		500 units per month	
	Total cost	Unit cost	Total cost	Unit cost
Materials (£10 per unit)	£1,000	£10	£5,000	£10
Labour (£5 per unit)	£500	£5	£2,500	£5
Overheads (£1,000 per month)	£1,000	£10	£1,000	£2
Total	£2,500	£25	£8,500	£17

Notice in this table that the total cost figures are based on the same ones that we calculated earlier, and that the unit cost is the same in total as we previously calculated.

In summary:

- to calculate **total costs**:
  multiply variable costs per unit by the output, and add to the fixed costs

- to calculate **unit costs:**
  divide the fixed costs by the output, and add to the variable costs per unit

We will now use a Case Study to make sure that we can deal with similar calculations when they are presented in a slightly different way.

Case Study

BEHAVE!
COST BEHAVIOUR CALCULATIONS

situation

'Behave!' is a dog training service that provides hour-long sessions to help owners control their pets. A unit of output for this organisation is one session.

The following table contains accurate data based on one month, and needs to be completed for various activity levels.

It has been established that stepped costs increase to £3,000 per month if the number of sessions is 200 or more.

Sessions	Stepped costs	Variable costs	Total costs	Unit cost
100	£2,000	£2,000	£4,000	£40
150				
200				
250				

required

Complete the table, showing stepped costs, variable costs, total costs and unit cost at the different activity levels (numbers of sessions). Show all amounts to the nearest £.

solution

Sessions	Stepped costs	Variable costs	Total costs	Unit cost
100	£2,000	£2,000	£4,000	£40
150	£2,000	£3,000	£5,000	£33
200	£3,000	£4,000	£7,000	£35
250	£3,000	£5,000	£8,000	£32

The calculations can be carried out as follows:

- the stepped costs are £2,000 per month for 100 and 150 sessions, but increase to £3,000 per month for 200 and 250 sessions

- the variable cost per unit can be calculated from the variable cost that is given, divided by the number of sessions, £2,000 ÷ 100 = £20; this can be used to calculate all the figures in the variable cost column by multiplying by the appropriate number of sessions (eg 150 sessions x £20 = £3,000).

- the total costs are calculated by adding the stepped and variable costs together

- the unit cost is calculated by dividing the total cost by the appropriate number of sessions (eg £5,000 ÷ 150 = £33)

PRODUCT COSTS AND PERIOD COSTS

You may be asked to distinguish between the terms 'product cost' and 'period cost'.

The total cost of a product is known as the product cost. This will be made up of different costs that behave in various ways (for example variable, semi-variable, and fixed or stepped). Throughout this chapter, we have seen how to calculate product costs.

Period costs are costs that relate to a period of time. For example, the monthly rent would be considered a period cost. As we have seen, period costs behave as fixed costs, or the fixed part of a cost. Period costs are often a part of the total product cost.

Chapter Summary

- Cost behaviour examines how costs respond to changes in the level of output or activity. Costs can behave in one of several ways, including as fixed costs, stepped costs, variable costs, and semi-variable costs.

- An understanding of cost behaviour can be used to enable the calculation of total costs and unit costs using simple arithmetic.

Key Terms

cost behaviour	the way that costs alter with changes in the level of output or activity
fixed cost	a cost that does not alter in total when the level of output or activity changes
stepped cost	a cost that is fixed within a range of output or activity levels, but changes to a different fixed level when outside that range
variable cost	a cost that changes in proportion to the level of output or activity
semi-variable cost	a cost that contains both a fixed element and a variable element

Activities

3.1   Identify the following statements as either true or false by putting a tick in the relevant column of the table below.

	True	False
Variable costs always include a time period cost		
Fixed costs are based on a time period and the amount does not depend on output		
Semi-variable costs change directly with changes in the level of activity		

3.2   Identify the following statements as either true or false by putting a tick in the relevant column of the table below.

	True	False
A variable cost is based on a unit of output and is the same for each one		
A total fixed cost changes as the level of activity increases		
A semi-variable cost is based on a combination of a time period cost and a per unit cost		

3.3   Classify the following costs as either fixed or variable by putting a tick in the relevant column of the table.

Costs	Fixed	Variable
Rent of premises		
Labour paid per unit produced		
Staff salaries		
Packaging materials for goods produced		

3.4   Classify the following costs as either fixed or variable by putting a tick in the relevant column of the table below.

Costs	Fixed	Variable
Insurance of vehicles		
Heating and lighting		
Materials used in production		
Bonus paid to production workers for each extra unit of output		

3.5   You work in the costing section of Doorcraft Ltd, a company that manufactures wooden doors. Each door is made by cutting up wood using a powered saw, and the wood pieces are screwed together. The door is then machine sanded and finally polished by hand.

Classify the following costs incurred by their behaviour (fixed, variable or semi-variable) by putting a tick in the relevant column of the table below.

Costs	Fixed	Variable	Semi-variable
Factory rates			
Power for saw and sanders in factory (charged per unit of electricity)			
Factory supervisors' wages (paid a time rate plus a production-based bonus)			
Wood used in the production process			
Telephone (charged at a flat rate plus an amount per call)			
Office rent			
Polish for finishing doors			
Delivery drivers' pay (paid a time rate plus a bonus per door delivered)			
Factory lighting			
Wages of production staff who are paid according to the number of doors they make			
Salary of marketing manager			

3.6   The following table contains data based on a company that makes a single product, and needs to be completed for different levels of production.

Output (units)	Fixed costs £	Variable costs £	Total costs £	Unit cost £
1,000	30,000	20,000	50,000	50
1,500				
2,000				
3,000				

You are to complete the table, showing fixed costs, variable costs, total costs and unit cost for the different levels of production.

3.7   Complete the table below showing fixed costs, variable costs, total costs and unit cost for the different levels of production.

Output (units)	Fixed costs £	Variable costs £	Total costs £	Unit cost £
2,000	12,000	4,000	16,000	8
3,000				
4,000				
6,000				

3.8   Complete the table below showing stepped costs, variable costs, total costs and unit cost for the different levels of production.

The stepped costs increase to £10,000 for output of 2,000 units or more.

Output (units)	Stepped costs £	Variable costs £	Total costs £	Unit cost £.p
500	8,000	2,000	10,000	20.00
1,000				
2,000				
4,000				

3.9 Victoria Ltd is costing a single product which has the following cost details:

Variable costs per unit

Material	£5
Labour	£4
Total fixed costs	£50,000

Complete the following total cost and unit cost table for a production level of 25,000 units.

	Total cost £	Unit cost £
Material		
Labour		
Overheads		
Total		

3.10 Albert Ltd is costing a single product which has the following cost details:

Variable costs per unit

Material	£10
Labour	£8
Total fixed costs	£90,000

Complete the following total cost and unit cost table for a production level of 30,000 units.

	Total cost £	Unit cost £
Material		
Labour		
Overheads		
Total		

4 Inventory valuation and the manufacturing account

this chapter covers...

In this chapter we will explain inventory (also called 'stock') held by an organisation – how it is classified, valued, and used to help calculate important costing information.

We will start by looking at inventory held by a manufacturing organisation and how it can be classified as it passes through the production process as:

- *raw materials*
- *part-finished goods (work-in-progress)*
- *finished goods*

We will then go on to describe the valuation methods that can be used by an organisation. As cost prices vary from time-to-time, organisations need to establish a policy of how goods which may have been bought at different times are to be valued.

The three methods of inventory valuation which we will examine and use are:

- *'first in first out' (FIFO)*
- *'last in first out' (LIFO), and*
- *'weighted average cost' (AVCO)*

We will describe how these methods work, and how they can be used to value inventory.

We then examine how inventory can be controlled using buffer stocks, re-order quantities and timings.

The final section of this chapter deals with the preparation of a manufacturing account which is a cost statement that shows the build up of costs, using valuations of raw materials, work-in-progress and finished goods.

TYPES OF INVENTORY

Inventory (also called 'stock') is held by a range of businesses.

■ **trading organisations**, such as shops, that simply buy and then sell the same items – this is their 'inventory'

■ **manufacturers** – businesses that manufacture products will hold inventory in various forms:

– **raw materials** – these are the materials that have been bought by a manufacturing business and are ready to be transferred to the production area where they will be used to make the finished goods

– **work-in-progress** – this comprises **part-finished products** that are awaiting completion

– **finished goods** – as the name suggests, these are manufactured items that have been completed and are ready for sale

In your studies you may be asked to classify inventory held by manufacturing businesses into the above three categories based on their descriptions, as in the following Case Study.

Case Study

TYPES OF INVENTORY

situation

Each item in the following table needs to be classified into one of the following three categories: raw materials or work-in-progress or finished goods.

Inventory item and organisation	Classification
Flour held by a pizza manufacturer	
Onions held by a pizza manufacturer	
New cars held by a car manufacturer	
Sheet steel held by a car manufacturer	
Car bodies manufactured by a car manufacturer awaiting completion	
Pizza bases (without toppings) held by a pizza manufacturer	
Pizzas held by a pizza manufacturer	

The answer is on the next page.

solution

Inventory item and organisation	Classification
Flour held by a pizza manufacturer	raw materials
Onions held by a pizza manufacturer	raw materials
New cars held by a car manufacturer	finished goods
Sheet steel held by a car manufacturer	raw materials
Car bodies manufactured by a car manufacturer awaiting completion	work-in-progress
Pizza bases (without toppings) held by a pizza manufacturer	work-in-progress
Pizzas held by a pizza manufacturer	finished goods

INVENTORY VALUATION

the need for valuation

It is important to know how inventory can be valued because the valuation is used in the calculation of:

- the cost of items that have been used in the production process to make a finished product

- the cost of items that remain

These costs will eventually be needed, in the case of a business, in the calculation of profit. In this chapter we will describe the different ways in which raw materials can be valued in the **manufacturing** process.

The process that we will be considering is split into three stages:

1 raw materials for the manufacturing process are bought from a supplier at a quoted purchase price

2 these materials are then stored on the premises (in a store area or warehouse) until needed for production

3 the goods are transferred to the production process when required

This process is illustrated in the diagram at the top of the next page.

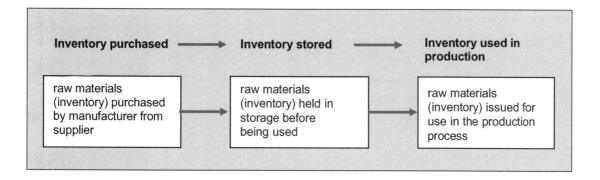

We are mainly concerned with the middle part of this diagram – the 'stores' section of the business. We need to know how materials that have been purchased can be valued.

the problem with valuation

If buying prices are always the same every time raw materials are bought then the same purchase price could be used for valuations and life would be simple.

The problem arises because **purchase prices change from time to time**, so inventory held in the stores may well be bought in at different prices, which makes valuation of that inventory difficult.

Is the valuation based on the most recent price paid? Or the price of the oldest inventory in the stores? Or even an average price of all the different prices paid for the same type of inventory?

In the next section we will describe three commonly used different methods of inventory valuation.

VALUATION METHODS

There are three main methods of valuing inventory. These are normally known by their abbreviations:

- FIFO (first in, first out)

- LIFO (last in, first out)

- AVCO (average cost)

We will explain and illustrate these.

■ **FIFO (First In, First Out)**

Using this method, the purchase price of the inventory that has been in the stores the longest is used to value the inventory that is issued from the stores – **first in, first out**.

This means that the inventory left in the stores is valued at the most recent cost prices.

■ **LIFO (Last In, First Out)**

The principle used is quite different from FIFO because the valuation of the inventory issued is based on the cost of the inventory most recently purchased – **last in first out**.

This means that the inventory left in the stores is valued at the older cost prices.

■ **AVCO (Average Cost)**

In this method, an overall **average cost** (or **average weighted cost**) is calculated for the inventory held in the stores, using the formula:

$$\text{average cost} = \frac{\text{total cost of goods in stores}}{\text{number of items in stores}}$$

This average cost is then used to value the inventory issued from the stores. This also means that a new average cost must be calculated each time that a new purchase of inventory is made.

We will now illustrate FIFO, LIFO and AVCO with a numerical example to explain how each system works. Then in the section that follows we will describe the characteristics and features of the three valuation methods.

We will take as an example a manufacturing business which buys in raw materials, stores the raw materials and then releases the raw materials to the manufacturing process.

The raw materials (inventory) in this illustration are in 'units'. In reality they could be kilos of chemicals, metres of cloth, litres of oil – or whatever raw materials the business in question uses to make its product.

The table at the top of the next page shows the quantities of units as they are purchased, stored and released for production:

■ **Receipts:** here there are two purchases of inventory

■ **Issues:** there is one issue of inventory

■ **Balance:** this shows the number of units of inventory left in the stores after each transaction (in reality there would be an 'opening balance' but this is omitted here for the sake of simplicity)

Receipts	Issues	Balance
Quantity	Quantity	Quantity
100		100
150		250
	80	170

You can see from this table that it works on the basis of a running account with the balance in the right hand column. The figures involved are:

- Purchases: 100 units + 150 units = 250 units in the store

- Issues: 250 units – 80 units = 170 units left in the store

We will now expand this table to include money amounts so that we can work out the value of inventory, using the three methods of FIFO, LIFO and AVCO. The purchases made were:100 units @ £40 per unit and 150 units @ £35 per unit.

FIFO (First In, First Out)

Using FIFO we assume that the inventory was issued in the order that it was bought. This would value the inventory issued to production at £40 per unit, and value the inventory still in stock partly at £40 per unit and partly at £35 per unit. The following table shows the values as well as quantities in all three columns.

FIFO

Receipts			Issues			Balance	
Quantity	Cost per unit	Total cost	Quantity	Value per unit	Total value	Quantity	Total value
100	£40	£4,000				100	£4,000
150	£35	£5,250				250	£9,250
			80	£40	£3,200	170	£6,050

This method values the issues in this example at £40 per unit x 80 units = £3,200.

That leaves the balance held with a value of £9,250 – £3,200 = £6,050.

This value is equal to the inventory remaining from each purchase:

From the first purchase	(100 – 80) = 20 units x £40 =	£800
From the second purchase	150 units x £35 =	£5,250
		————
Total		£6,050
		————

LIFO (Last In, First Out)

LIFO is different from FIFO because the valuation of the inventory issued is based on the cost of the inventory most **recently** purchased and not the oldest purchase.

This method would value the inventory issued to production at £35 per unit and value the inventory still in stock partly at £40 per unit and partly at £35 per unit, although in different proportions to the last method. The following table shows how these values would appear.

LIFO

Receipts			Issues			Balance	
Quantity	Cost per unit	Total cost	Quantity	Value per unit	Total value	Quantity	Total value
100	£40	£4,000				100	£4,000
150	£35	£5,250				250	£9,250
			80	£35	£2,800	170	£6,450

This method values the issues in this example at £35 per unit x 80 units = £2,800.

That leaves the balance held with a value of £9,250 – £2,800 = £6,450.

This value is equal to the inventory remaining from each purchase:

From the first purchase	100 units x £40 =	£4,000
From the second purchase (150 – 80) =	70 units x £35 =	£2,450
Total		£6,450

AVCO (Average Cost)

As we have already seen, when using the AVCO method of valuation, an overall average cost is calculated for the inventory held in the stores, using the formula:

$$\text{average cost} = \frac{\text{total cost of goods in stores}}{\text{number of items in stores}}$$

In the example we are using, we will work out the average cost of the inventory when it was purchased, and then use that average cost for both the next issue (80 units) and also the balance of inventory remaining (170 units).

The average value per unit is calculated as £9,250 ÷ 250 units = £37 per unit (see the table below).

AVCO

Receipts			Issues			Balance	
Quantity	Cost per unit	Total cost	Quantity	Value per unit	Total value	Quantity	Total value
100	£40	£4,000				100	£4,000
150	£35	£5,250				250	£9,250
			80	£37	£2,960	170	£6,290

AVCO values the issues in this example at £37 per unit x 80 units = £2,960.

That leaves the balance held in the stores with a value of £9,250 – £2,960 = £6,290.

This value is equal to 170 units x £37 = £6,290.

Note that the unit value worked out to an exact amount in this example. Sometimes rounding of the final issues and balance values will be required.

inventory valuations – summary

Each method of valuation will give a different answer, but each method is equally valid. In the example given we probably would not know which delivery of inventory was actually used for the issue, but that does not matter. The three inventory valuations methods are based on making assumptions about the way that inventory is used up, but these assumptions are only for valuation purposes – it is not relevant if the goods are actually used in that order or not.

CHARACTERISTICS OF INVENTORY VALUATION METHODS

The table below summarises the key characteristics of the three methods of inventory valuation that we have examined.

CHARACTERISTICS OF INVENTORY VALUATION METHODS			
	FIFO	**LIFO**	**AVCO**
VALUATION OF ISSUES Issues of inventory are valued at the oldest purchase prices	✓		
Issues of inventory are valued at the most recent purchase prices		✓	
Issues of inventory are valued at the weighted average cost of purchases			✓
VALUATION OF INVENTORY BALANCE Inventory balance is valued at the most recent purchase costs	✓		
Inventory balance is valued at the oldest purchase costs		✓	
Inventory balance is valued at the weighted average cost of purchases			✓

The previous table, together with what you have learned earlier about FIFO, LIFO and AVCO, will enable you to answer true or false statements which may be asked in assessments. Try the following statements by putting a tick in the relevant column of the table (answers are at the bottom of the page):

	True	False
1. FIFO costs issues of inventory in the opposite order to which it was received		
2. AVCO costs issues of inventory in the same order to which it was received		
3. LIFO costs issues of inventory at the latest purchase prices		
4. LIFO values closing inventory at the oldest purchase prices		
5. FIFO values closing inventory at the most recent purchase costs		
6. AVCO values closing inventory at the weighted average cost of purchases		

choosing an inventory valuation method

A business will need to decide which method of inventory valuation it will use. Although the examples we have used show the effect of using each method of inventory valuation, a business would make a decision as to which method is most appropriate for its needs, and then use it consistently.

Note that the LIFO method can only be used for internal costing purposes, and cannot be used for financial accounting.

Answers: 1. False; 2. False; 3. True; 4. True; 5. True; 6. True

CALCULATION OF INVENTORY VALUATIONS

In the examples of inventory valuation on pages 72-75, we used two purchases and one issue to illustrate each of the three methods. In the Case Study which follows on the next page we will present a practical example of these calculations.

This time we will provide an opening balance of inventory held, which adds another step to the calculation process. The principle is exactly the same as the presentation of any running balance account, such as shown in a bank statement: you start with a balance, enter 'in' and 'out' transactions and finish with a balance.

The key to accurate valuation calculations is to work through the figures from the earliest transaction to the latest, carrying out the required valuations of issues and balances in strict date order. This means that:

■ where there is a starting balance and valuation, it is used in conjunction with the next purchase or issue to calculate the next balance and its valuation

■ where purchases are made, the new balance is calculated and valued using the previous balance and adding in the quantity and value of the purchase

■ where issues are made, the quantity is deducted from the previous inventory balance, and the issue valuation is deducted from the previous inventory valuation

Using this logical approach you will find that the arithmetic works for both **quantities** and **values**:

opening inventory of raw materials	**plus**	purchases of raw materials	**minus**	issues of raw materials	**equals**	closing inventory of raw materials

This is a useful check that your calculations make sense.

It is also important to use clear and accurate workings, so that you can easily see which values apply to which quantities. These workings could be inserted into a table (as is carried out in the next Case Study) or placed elsewhere if there is no room.

FUEL STOP:
INVENTORY VALUATION METHODS

situation

The Fuel Stop is a garage that buys fuel in bulk, and sells it to passing motorists. The fuel is held in a large tank, and deliveries are arranged so that the tank does not run dry. The following table shows a summary of the order of movements in fuel inventory during one week in litres.

Receipts (Purchases)			Issues (Sales)			Balance		
Quantity	Cost per litre	Total cost	Quantity	Value per litre	Total value	Quantity	Value per litre	Total value
						2,000	£0.90	£1,800
10,000	£1.20	£12,000						
			8,000					

required

Set up three tables to calculate valuations of issues, and quantities and valuations of all balances, using:

(a)   FIFO (First in first out) valuation

(b)   LIFO (Last in first out) valuation

(c)   AVCO (Average cost) valuation

solution – FIFO

The table appears as follows:

Receipts (Purchases)			Issues (Sales)			Balance		
Quantity	Cost per litre	Total cost	Quantity	Value per litre	Total value	Quantity	Value per litre	Total value
						2,000	£0.90	£1,800
10,000	£1.20	£12,000				2,000	£0.90	£1,800
						10,000	£1.20	£12,000
						————		————
						12,000		£13,800
			2,000	£0.90	£1,800	4,000	£1.20	£4,800
			6,000	£1.20	£7,200			
			————		————			
			8,000		£9,000			

Study the order and workings for the calculations in this solution. The following is a summary of what has taken place:

- Note that there is an opening balance of 2,000 litres, valued at £1,800 (90p per litre).

- The receipt of 10,000 litres at £1.20 is added to the opening balance, but the make-up of the value of the new balance is clearly shown so that the earliest part can be used first for the next issue.

- The issue of 8,000 litres is split into 2,000 litres and 6,000 litres to agree with the order of arrival of the petrol within the previous balance. This logic is continued in the calculation of the new balance, and we can see that all the litres at £0.90 have gone, and only 4,000 litres are left at £1.20 per litre, which represents the remaining part of the last receipt.

The arithmetic for both quantities and values is as follows:

	Quantities (litres)	Values (£)
Opening inventory balance	2,000	1,800
+ Purchases	10,000	12,000
- Issues	(8,000)	(9,000)
= Closing inventory balance	4,000	4,800

solution – LIFO

The table appears as follows:

Receipts (Purchases)			Issues (Sales)			Balance		
Quantity	Cost per litre	Total cost	Quantity	Value per litre	Total value	Quantity	Value per litre	Total value
						2,000	£0.90	£1,800
10,000	£1.20	£12,000				2,000	£0.90	£1,800
						10,000	£1.20	£12,000
						12,000		£13,800
			8,000	£1.20	£9,600	2,000	£0.90	£1,800
						2,000	£1.20	£2,400
						4,000		£4,200

- Note that there is an opening balance of 2,000 litres, valued at £1,800 (90p per litre).

- The issue of 8,000 litres is not split, since the whole amount is matched against the most recent purchase of 10,000 litres. This leaves a balance which is split into 2,000 litres at £0.90 and 2,000 litres at £1.20.

The arithmetic for both quantities and values is as follows:

	Quantities (litres)	Values (£)
Opening inventory balance	2,000	£1,800
+ Purchases	10,000	£12,000
- Issues	(8,000)	(£9,600)
= Closing inventory balance	4,000	£4,200

solution – AVCO

The table appears as follows:

Receipts (Purchases)			Issues (Sales)			Balance		
Quantity	Cost per litre	Total cost	Quantity	Value per litre	Total value	Quantity	Value per litre	Total value
						2,000	£0.90	£1,800
10,000	£1.20	£12,000				2,000		£1,800
						10,000		£12,000
						12,000	£1.15	£13,800
			8,000	£1.15	£9,200	4,000	£1.15	£4,600

The AVCO valuation method requires a slightly different technique to the other two.

There is no need to keep track of each purchase, since each time more goods are received a new average cost is calculated. This average is used for issues and balances until more goods are purchased.

These are the calculation methods used:

- When the purchase is made, an average cost is calculated by adding separately the quantities and values, and then dividing the total value by the total quantity to arrive at an average value per litre.

  In this example the calculation is £13,800 ÷ 12,000 litres = £1.15 per litre.

- The £1.15 per litre is then used to value the next issue and also the remaining balance.

The overall calculation is as follows:

	Quantities (litres)	Values (£)
Opening inventory balance	2,000	1,800
+ Purchases	10,000	12,000
- Issues	(8,000)	(9,200)
= Closing inventory balance	4,000	4,600

CONTROL OF INVENTORY LEVELS

Organisations should make sure that they hold an appropriate level of inventory of the various materials that they need. If they hold too much inventory, they risk storage and cash flow problems. If they hold too little inventory, they may run out and bring production to a halt.

An organisation may draw up an **inventory control policy** to help manage the inventory level. This policy may include reference to the following terms, which we need to understand.

- **buffer stock** (or inventory buffer)

  This is the extra amount of inventory that is held as a contingency (a reserve) in case things do not go according to plan and there is a danger that inventory may run out. The amount of buffer stock will be determined by the organisation.

- **lead time**

  This is the length of time between placing an order to purchase more material, and it actually arriving. This will be based on negotiation between the organisation and the supplier and will be affected by the geographical location of the supplier.

- **re-order level**

  When the inventory level drops to the re-order level, then it is time to place an order for more material. This will be calculated based on the average usage (ie issues) of the material and the lead time, so that by the time the inventory reaches the buffer stock, the new order arrives.

- **re-order quantity**

  This is the amount of material that should be ordered each time that an order is placed. This will be decided so that there are not too many orders needed, but there is enough space to keep the materials. If the order arrives, as planned, when the buffer stock level has just been reached, then the new inventory level will normally be the maximum inventory level.

The following diagram shows how the system works.

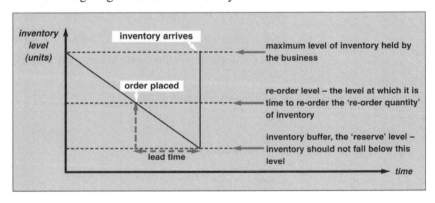

You may be asked to analyse and report on compliance with an inventory control policy. The following Case Study looks at this situation.

JUST ENOUGH LIMITED
INVENTORY CONTROL COMPLIANCE

situation

Just Enough Limited has set the following levels and timings as part of its policy for control of the inventory of one of its raw materials:

Buffer Stock (Inventory Buffer)	4,000 kilos
Lead Time	7 days
Re-order Level	11,000 kilos
Re-order Quantity	20,000 kilos

The normal daily usage (issues) of the raw material is 1,000 kilos, and the re-order level has been determined based on this, together with the established lead time.

Examine the following alternative situations where the policy is not followed. You have been asked to calculate the inventory levels immediately before and after the order is received, and to comment on the implications of each alternative. Assume that the lead time is maintained, and the daily issues are as expected.

(a) An order for 20,000 kilos is placed 3 days before the re-order level is expected to be reached, instead of at the re-order level.

(b) An order for 20,000 kilos is placed 5 days after the re-order level was reached, instead of at the re-order level.

(c) An order for 10,000 kilos is placed when the inventory reached the re-order level.

(d) An order for 40,000 kilos is placed when the inventory reached the re-order level.

solution

(a) Based on usage of 1,000 kilos per day, the inventory level would be 3,000 kilos higher than the buffer stock level of 4,000 kilos just before the order arrives. It would therefore be 7,000 kilos. After the delivery, the inventory would be 7,000 kilos + 20,000 kilos = 27,000 kilos. This is higher than the usual maximum inventory level, and this may cause storage problems. Payment for the materials may need to be made earlier than expected due to the early delivery.

(b) Since the buffer stock of 4,000 kilos is equivalent to 4 days' usage, the business will have run out of inventory a day before the order is delivered. This may have brought production to a halt. The inventory level will therefore be zero before the order is delivered, and 20,000 kilos immediately afterwards.

(c) If the order placed is for only 10,000 kilos, the inventory level will be 4,000 kilos immediately before delivery (the normal buffer level), and 14,000 kilos afterwards. This is below the expected maximum inventory. The next order will need to be placed 10 days earlier than normal since this delivery will be used up more quickly, and the re-order level reached sooner.

(d) If the order placed is for 40,000 kilos, the inventory level will be 4,000 kilos immediately before delivery (the normal buffer level), and 44,000 kilos afterwards. This is well above the expected maximum inventory, and this may cause storage space problems. The increased size of the order may cause cash flow problems as the payment will be for twice the normal amount. The next order will need to be placed 20 days later than normal since this delivery will take longer to be used up, and the re-order level will be reached later.

USING INVENTORY VALUATIONS

Earlier in this chapter we learned how to identify the different types of inventory. For a manufacturing business these are raw materials, work-in-progress (part-finished goods), and finished goods. The inventory valuations for these are used in the calculation of summary figures needed by a manufacturing business.

The summary figures of a manufacturing business are:

- direct materials used
- direct cost
- manufacturing cost
- cost of goods manufactured
- cost of goods sold

These are calculated for a period of time (for example a week, month or year), through the use of a cost statement called a 'manufacturing account'. We will now look in detail at what each summary figure means, and how it is calculated, and then put the information together in the manufacturing account format.

direct materials used

The term **direct materials** is one that we have used earlier in this book, and describes materials that can be identified directly with the units of output. We are going to consider a manufacturing business where the direct materials are all raw materials.

When we examined valuation methods, we noticed that raw materials are not always used immediately in manufacture, but are often stored for a time as inventory. The total figure that we need to calculate as direct materials used is equivalent to the valuation of issues from stores to production. The easiest way to calculate the amount of direct materials used is to follow the formula seen earlier (page 78) for raw materials:

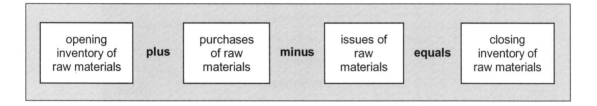

This is the same as:

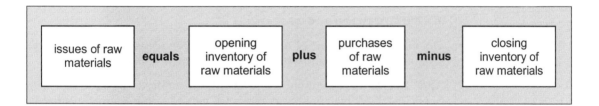

In other words, the amount of raw materials used in production is made up of the amount of inventory at the beginning of the period, plus the amount purchased, less the amount that forms the closing inventory.

We therefore have a straightforward way to calculate the value of the direct materials used. The calculation forms the first part of the manufacturing account format and appears as follows. Sample figures have been inserted to illustrate the calculation.

Opening inventory of raw materials	£20,000
Purchases of raw materials	+ £40,000
Closing inventory of raw materials	− £15,000
DIRECT MATERIALS USED	= £45,000

It is important to note that the closing inventory valuation is always deducted in the calculation. (The symbols for '+', '−' and '=' are given in these examples to guide you, although they may not be given in assessments and activities.)

direct cost

This is the total of all direct costs (costs that can be directly identified with units of output). You will recall that the elements of cost are materials, labour and expenses. Since direct expenses are not very common, we are going to assume in our manufacturing account that direct cost consists only of direct materials used, plus direct labour. We can therefore build on our earlier manufacturing account format as follows, again using sample figures.

Opening inventory of raw materials	£20,000
Purchases of raw materials	+ £40,000
Closing inventory of raw materials	– £15,000
DIRECT MATERIALS USED	= £45,000
Direct labour	+ £35,000
DIRECT COST	= £80,000

manufacturing cost

The manufacturing cost of a product is made up of its direct cost and the manufacturing overheads associated with making that product.

After adding manufacturing overheads, the manufacturing cost statement comprises direct materials used, direct labour and manufacturing overheads. We then sub-total these to give a figure that may be called manufacturing cost. However, in order to calculate the cost of goods manufactured we first need to adjust for the inventory valuation of work-in-progress.

cost of goods manufactured

Cost of goods manufactured means the total costs of running the factory. It is calculated from direct cost by:

- adding the manufacturing overheads, which are the indirect costs of running the factory

- adjusting for work-in-progress at the beginning and end of the accounting period

Work-in-progress is any part-completed goods that may be in the factory at the beginning and at the end of the accounting period. For example, at any one time a car manufacturer will have partly-assembled cars going down the production line. It is the valuation of such partly-completed goods that gives the figure for work-in-progress – both at the beginning and at the end of the accounting period.

The adjustment for work-in-progress is made after the sub-total figure for manufacturing cost and we must:

■ add opening inventory of work-in-progress

■ deduct closing inventory of work-in-progress

To summarise this part of the manufacturing account, starting with the figure for direct cost:

■ add manufacturing overheads

■ sub-total for manufacturing cost

■ add opening inventory of work-in-progress

■ deduct closing inventory of work-in-progress

■ sub-total for cost of goods manufactured

We can therefore see how the information using sample figures is building up in our manufacturing account format:

Opening inventory of raw materials	£20,000
Purchases of raw materials	+ £40,000
Closing inventory of raw materials	− £15,000
DIRECT MATERIALS USED	= £45,000
Direct labour	+ £35,000
DIRECT COST	= £80,000
Manufacturing overheads	+ £18,000
MANUFACTURING COST	= £98,000
Opening inventory of work-in-progress	+ £11,000
Closing inventory of work-in-progress	− £14,000
COST OF GOODS MANUFACTURED	= £95,000

Note that the closing inventory of work-in-progress is a deduction, in the same way that the closing inventory of raw materials is a deduction.

cost of goods sold

This is the final summary total, and it may be used in the calculation of profit by comparing it with the sales revenue. Cost of goods sold (also known as the cost of sales) must take account of the third category of inventory – finished goods. Cost of goods sold is made up of the value of the finished goods that existed at the start of the period, plus the cost of goods manufactured, but excluding the value of the finished goods inventory that remains at the end of the period. We therefore adjust the earlier total of cost of goods manufactured and:

■ add opening inventory of finished goods

■ deduct closing inventory of finished goods

The complete statement of a manufacturing account format now appears as follows, using the earlier sample figures, plus those for finished goods inventories:

Opening inventory of raw materials	£20,000
Purchases of raw materials	+ £40,000
Closing inventory of raw materials	– £15,000
DIRECT MATERIALS USED	= £45,000
Direct labour	+ £35,000
DIRECT COST	= £80,000
Manufacturing overheads	+ £18,000
MANUFACTURING COST	= £98,000
Opening inventory of work-in-progress	+ £11,000
Closing inventory of work-in-progress	– £14,000
COST OF GOODS MANUFACTURED	= £95,000
Opening inventory of finished goods	+ £17,000
Closing inventory of finished goods	– £16,000
COST OF GOODS SOLD	= £96,000

As noted earlier the symbols for '+', '–' and '=' are given to guide you, although they may not be given in assessments and activities.

We will now use a Case Study to practise preparing the manufacturing account format.

MAKEM LIMITED:
MANUFACTURING ACCOUNT FORMAT

situation

You are employed by Makem Limited, a manufacturing company. A trainee has produced a list of data that needs to be assembled into a manufacturing account format. All the data has been checked for accuracy.

You are to reorder the following costs into a manufacturing account format for the year ended 31 December 20-1. Make sure that the arithmetic of your manufacturing account format is accurate.

DIRECT COST	£74,000
Opening inventory of raw materials	£12,000
Direct labour	£39,000
Closing inventory of finished goods	£15,000
COST OF GOODS SOLD	£98,000
Purchases of raw materials	£37,000
Opening inventory of finished goods	£19,000
MANUFACTURING COST	£97,000
Closing inventory of work-in-progress	£13,000
Opening inventory of work-in-progress	£10,000
Closing inventory of raw materials	£14,000
DIRECT MATERIALS USED	£35,000
Manufacturing overheads	£23,000
COST OF GOODS MANUFACTURED	£94,000

solution

Manufacturing account format for the year ended 31 December 20-1	
Opening inventory of raw materials	£12,000
Purchases of raw materials	£37,000
Closing inventory of raw materials	£14,000
DIRECT MATERIALS USED	£35,000
Direct labour	£39,000
DIRECT COST	£74,000
Manufacturing overheads	£23,000
MANUFACTURING COST	£97,000
Opening inventory of work-in-progress	£10,000
Closing inventory of work-in-progress	£13,000
COST OF GOODS MANUFACTURED	£94,000
Opening inventory of finished goods	£19,000
Closing inventory of finished goods	£15,000
COST OF GOODS SOLD	£98,000

Note that the symbols for '+', '–' and '=' have not been shown. For practise, you may like to show them before checking the accuracy of the arithmetic.

Chapter Summary

- Inventories are held by manufacturing businesses in various forms – raw materials, work-in-progress and finished goods.

- A decision needs to be made on the method of inventory valuation that is to be used for raw materials. This is because inventory is made up of items bought at different prices and an assumption needs to be made for valuation purposes about the order that they are used up.

- The three main methods of inventory valuation for raw materials are:

  - first in first out (FIFO)

  - last in first out (LIFO)

  - average cost (AVCO)

Each method involves calculating the value of issues and the remaining balance in different ways.

- Inventory levels can be managed by using an inventory control policy which includes details of buffer stocks, lead times, re-order levels, and re-order quantities.

- Manufacturing accounts are used by businesses that produce goods to summarise the cost data for a period of time. The accounts are prepared in an established format and provide valuable information about the total costs at various stages. Manufacturing accounts use inventory valuations for raw materials, work-in-progress and finished goods at appropriate points to ensure that the information produced is valid and useful.

Key Terms

raw materials	the materials bought by manufacturing organisations and used to manufacture the finished products
work-in-progress	the name given to partly-completed items in a manufacturing organisation
finished goods	the items that have been manufactured and are ready for sale
first in first out (FIFO)	a method of inventory valuation that assumes that goods will be used up in the order that they are acquired (for valuation purposes only). This means that the remaining balance will be valued based on the prices of more recent purchases
last in first out (LIFO)	this method of inventory valuation assumes that the most recently acquired inventory will be used first, leaving the earlier acquisitions to make up the value of the remaining balance. This does not have to correspond with the actual order of usage

average cost (AVCO)	this inventory valuation method involves calculating a new weighted average cost of goods each time that a new purchase is made, and using this valuation for subsequent issues and balances until further purchases are made
inventory control policy	an organisation's plan to manage inventory levels
buffer stock (inventory buffer)	an amount of inventory held in reserve in case things do not go to plan
lead time	the time between placing an order for further supplies, and the goods arriving
re-order level	when inventory falls to this level, a new order should be placed
re-order quantity	the quantity of materials that should be ordered each time
manufacturing account	this cost statement is produced at the end of a period to summarise costs under various categories
direct materials	this is calculated as the total of opening inventory of raw materials, plus materials purchased, minus closing inventory of raw materials
direct cost	the total of direct costs (also known as prime cost) – in a manufacturing account it is calculated by adding direct materials used in manufacture to direct labour
manufacturing cost	a subtotal made up of the total of direct cost (direct materials and direct labour) and manufacturing overheads
cost of goods manufactured	this subtotal is the production costs of goods that have been completed and is made up of manufacturing cost adjusted for inventories of work-in-progress
cost of goods sold	a total based on the factory cost of goods manufactured which has been adjusted for inventories of finished goods

Activities

4.1   You work for a training organisation, and have been asked to work out the answers for an exercise to be set for accountancy students. You are to classify each inventory item on the following list into one of the following categories:

- raw materials

- work-in-progress

- finished goods

List of inventory items for classification:

Inventory item and organisation	Classification
Wood held by a door manufacturer	
Flour held by a cake manufacturer	
Cakes awaiting icing held by a cake manufacturer	
Doors awaiting sanding and polishing held by a door manufacturer	
Flour held by a flour miller	
Wheat held by a flour miller	
Screws held by a screw manufacturer	
Screws held by a door manufacturer	

4.2   Identify the correct inventory valuation method from the characteristics given by putting a tick in the relevant column of the following table.

Characteristic	FIFO	LIFO	AVCO
Issues of inventory are valued at the weighted average cost of purchases			
Closing inventory is valued at the oldest purchase costs			
Issues of inventory are valued at the most recent purchase prices			
Closing inventory is valued at the weighted average cost of purchases			
Closing inventory is valued at the most recent purchase costs			
Issues of inventory are valued at the oldest purchase prices			

4.3 Indicate whether the following statements are true or false by putting a tick in the relevant columns of the table below.

	True	False
FIFO costs issues of inventory in the same order in which they were received		
FIFO values closing inventory based on the oldest purchase prices		
LIFO costs issues of inventory at the oldest purchase prices		
LIFO values closing inventory at the average cost of purchases		
AVCO costs issues of inventory at the most recent purchase prices		
AVCO values closing inventory at the weighted average cost of purchases		

4.4 Which **one** of the following is true for the FIFO method of inventory valuation?

(a) Issues are valued at the most recent purchase prices

(b) Inventory balance is valued at the average of the cost of purchases

(c) A new average cost is calculated each time a purchase is made

(d) Inventory balance is valued at the most recent purchase prices

Answer (a) or (b) or (c) or (d)

4.5 Which **one** of the following is true for the LIFO method of inventory valuation?

(a) The latest purchase costs are used to value issues

(b) Issues are valued at the average of the cost of purchases

(c) Inventory remaining at the end of the period is valued at the most recent purchase costs

(d) Issues are unlikely to be valued at the actual cost of purchase

Answer (a) or (b) or (c) or (d)

4.6 Which **one** of the following is true for the AVCO method of inventory valuation?

(a) Uses the oldest purchase costs to value issues

(b) Inventory balance is valued at the average of the cost of purchases

(c) Issues are valued at the most recent purchase prices

(d) Inventory remaining at the end of the period is valued at the oldest purchase costs

Answer (a) or (b) or (c) or (d)

4.7 Identify which **one** of the following inventory calculations is correct.

(a) Opening inventory, minus purchases, minus issues, equals closing inventory

(b) Purchases, minus issues, minus opening inventory, equals closing inventory

(c) Closing inventory plus opening inventory, equals purchases

(d) Opening inventory, plus purchases, minus issues, equals closing Inventory

Answer (a) or (b) or (c) or (d)

4.8 Identify which inventory valuation method is being used in the following situation. Choose between FIFO, LIFO, AVCO by ticking the box below.

Receipts			Issues			Balance	
Quantity (units)	Cost per unit	Total cost	Quantity (units)	Value per unit	Total value	Quantity (units)	Total value
100	£20	£2,000				100	£2,000
150	£25	£3,750				250	£5,750
			80	£23	£1,840	170	£3,910

FIFO	
LIFO	
AVCO	

4.9 The following table shows the movements in a certain type of inventory through a business's stores in February.

Date	Receipts		Issues	
	Units	Cost	Units	Cost
Feb 6	100	£600		
Feb 15	150	£1,200		
Feb 22	250	£2,500		
Feb 26			300	
Feb 27	200	£2,400		

Complete the table below for the issue on 26 February and closing inventory values at 28 February.

Method	Cost of issue on 26 February £	Closing inventory value at 28 February £
FIFO		
LIFO		
AVCO		

4.10 Wyvern Ltd has the following movements in a certain type of inventory into and out of its stores for the month of January:

Date	Receipts		Issues	
	Units	Cost	Units	Cost
3 January	100	£1,000		
14 January	200	£2,400		
20 January	100	£1,400		
22 January			150	
27 January	300	£4,500		

Complete the table below for the issue on 22 January and closing inventory values at 31 January.

Method	Cost of issue on 22 January £	Closing inventory value at 31 January £
FIFO		
LIFO		
AVCO		

4.11   Complete the tables below, using the FIFO, LIFO and AVCO methods of inventory valuation:

(a)   FIFO

Receipts			Issues			Balance		
Quantity (units)	Cost per unit	Total cost	Quantity (units)	Value per unit	Total value	Quantity (units)	Value per unit	Total value
						2,000	£2.02	£4,040
10,000	£2.20							
			8,000					

(b)   LIFO

Receipts			Issues			Balance		
Quantity (units)	Cost per unit	Total cost	Quantity (units)	Value per unit	Total value	Quantity (units)	Value per unit	Total value
						2,000	£2.02	£4,040
10,000	£2.20							
			8,000					

(c)   AVCO

Receipts			Issues			Balance		
Quantity (units)	Cost per unit	Total cost	Quantity (units)	Value per unit	Total value	Quantity (units)	Value per unit	Total value
						2,000	£2.02	£4,040
10,000	£2.20							
			8,000					

4.12   A company has the following data included in its inventory control policy:

Inventory buffer	10,000 units
Lead time	5 days
Re-order level	20,000 units
Re-order quantity	30,000 units

The daily usage of materials is always 2,000 units (7 days a week)

On 3rd May the inventory level was 34,000 units.

On 5th May an order was placed for 20,000 units.

The order arrived on 10th May.

Analyse the above information, comparing the control policy with the actual events. Tick which of the following statements are true.

Statement	True
The order was placed at the correct inventory level	
The order was placed early	
The order was placed late	
The amount ordered was correct	
The amount ordered was too much	
The amount ordered was too little	
The delivery arrived when the inventory reached the buffer level	
The delivery arrived when the inventory was above the buffer level	
The delivery arrived when the inventory was below the buffer level	

4.13 Reorder the following costs into a manufacturing account format on the right-hand side of the table below.

Make sure that the arithmetic of your account is accurate.

	£		£
DIRECT COST	79,000		
Opening inventory of raw materials	13,000		
Direct labour	30,000		
Closing inventory of finished goods	14,000		
COST OF GOODS SOLD	93,000		
Purchases of raw materials	47,000		
Opening inventory of finished goods	15,000		
MANUFACTURING COST	99,000		
Closing inventory of work-in-progress	19,000		
Opening inventory of work-in-progress	12,000		
Closing inventory of raw materials	11,000		
DIRECT MATERIALS USED	49,000		
Manufacturing overheads	20,000		
COST OF GOODS MANUFACTURED	92,000		

4.14 Reorder the following costs into a manufacturing account format on the right-hand side of the table below.

Make sure that the arithmetic of your account is accurate.

	£		£
Closing inventory of finished goods	32,000		
COST OF GOODS SOLD	178,000		
Manufacturing overheads	38,000		
Opening inventory of raw materials	15,000		
DIRECT MATERIALS USED	82,000		
Opening inventory of work-in-progress	26,000		
Direct labour	55,000		
MANUFACTURING COST	175,000		
Opening inventory of finished goods	37,000		
COST OF GOODS MANUFACTURED	173,000		
Purchases of raw materials	85,000		
Closing inventory of work-in-progress	28,000		
DIRECT COST	137,000		
Closing inventory of raw materials	18,000		

5 Labour costs

this chapter covers...

We have already seen that labour cost is one of the three main elements of cost, along with materials and expenses. In this chapter we will look in more detail at labour costs.

The chapter starts by examining the main ways that employees' pay can be calculated. These are:

- *payment based on the normal time worked – known as basic pay, or time-rate*

- *payment based on extra time worked – known as overtime*

- *payment of a bonus (individual or team)*

- *payment based on output – piecework*

- *piecework with guaranteed minimum payment*

We will examine features of each method, and carry out calculations.

We will then link this understanding of labour costs to our earlier work on cost classification and coding, with examples of how coding can be used for labour costs.

Finally we will refer to our earlier work on cost behaviour, and identify how the different methods of labour payment affect the behaviour of the labour cost.

METHODS OF CALCULATING PAYMENTS FOR LABOUR

The cost of labour for an organisation is the cost of paying employees for the work that they carry out. There are several different ways that these amounts can be calculated, and the details of the method that applies to each group of employees will have been formally agreed and set out in a contract of employment.

These are the main methods of calculating pay:

- **time rate** – payment based on time worked, also known as **basic rate**

- **overtime** – a form of time rate – payment for extra time worked

- payment of a **bonus** added onto the normal time rate and overtime

- **piecework** – payment based on the amount of work carried out

- piecework with guaranteed minimum payment

Organisations may use one method of payment for all employees or they may have different methods for different groups of employees.

We will now examine these main payment methods that you will need to be familiar with.

time rate

Time rate is based on payment for the amount of time spent working.

The unit of time is usually quoted as an hourly rate which is then multiplied by the hours worked but it could also be based on a weekly or monthly rate. Examples of time rate payments could be:

- a trainee accountant paid £1,500 per month

- a production supervisor paid £500 per week

- a production operator paid £12.00 per hour

In each case, the contract would state how much time would normally be spent working, for example 38 hours per week.

For both the employee and the organisation, pay based on a time rate means that it is known in advance how much will be paid. This makes planning easier for both employer and employee and gives the employees the security of knowing that they will be paid the same for each period at work.

However, just using this payment method means that efficient employees are paid the same as inefficient ones, and they receive no financial reward for working harder.

The amount paid per time period of normal working is known as the **basic rate**, and this term is commonly used for the normal hourly rate. For example, an employee may be paid a basic rate of £12.00 per hour for each of the 38 hours worked in a week, so they are paid £456 for the week.

overtime rate

An overtime rate is a time rate that is paid for time worked in excess of the normal contracted time.

An overtime rate (usually hourly) is invariably higher than the basic rate – for example, a basic rate of £12.00 and an overtime rate of £18.00 per hour. This may also be known as 'time and a half', since £18 is one and a half times £12. The difference between the basic rate and the overtime rate is also known as the overtime premium.

worked example

Suppose a production operative was entitled to a basic rate of £12.00 per hour, based on a 38 hour week, and an overtime rate of £18.00 per hour for any hours in excess of 38 hours. If during a certain week this person worked 42 hours, then the pay would be calculated as:

Basic rate	38 hours x £12.00	£456.00
Overtime rate	4 hours x £18.00	£72.00
Total		£528.00

bonus payments

A bonus payment is an extra payment paid to employees as a reward for productivity.

Bonus payments are normally offered to reward employees when the organisation performs well, either in term of output (items produced, products sold) or when sales and profit are good.

■ **individual bonus**

Bonus payments are based on a variety of calculations, but here we will concentrate on a simple approach based on the output achieved by the employee. This involves paying a bonus if the employee's work output (for example units of production) is greater than a certain amount. The bonus is calculated based on the extra amount produced.

worked example

Suppose an employee is paid a basic rate of £10.00 per hour for a 35 hour week. A weekly bonus is paid if the average production of an employee is more than 4 units per hour. For every unit produced by the employee in excess of 4 units per hour a bonus of £1.20 is payable.

Suppose that during a certain week an employee works 35 hours and produces 170 units.

The bonus would be calculated as follows:

Actual output	170 units
Expected output (35 hours x 4 units)	140 units
Excess output that earns bonus	30 units
Bonus payable 30 units x £1.20 = £36.00	

This bonus would be paid in addition to the amount paid at the time rate:

Basic rate 35 hours x £10.00	£350.00
Bonus (as calculated above)	£36.00
Total pay	£386.00

If the employee had produced 140 units or fewer then no bonus would be paid, and the person would just receive the time rate based amount. There would be no reduction in pay (or 'negative bonus') for producing fewer than the expected number of units.

A production based bonus system used in conjunction with payment by time rate gives employees the security to know that their pay will not fall below the time-based amount. It also encourages productive working which is beneficial for both employees and the organisation.

■ **team bonus**

Where employees work in teams, a bonus scheme could be used to motivate and reward everyone in the team. The scheme would use the whole team's performance to determine a bonus, and then this would be shared among the employees in the team. A team bonus scheme may be appropriate where employees' output cannot be measured individually, and where teamwork is to be encouraged.

worked example

A team of six forestry workers are employed to cut down selected trees, cut the timber into specified lengths, and load it onto trucks.

Each team member is paid £12 per hour for a forty-hour week plus a share in a team bonus. A bonus of £50 per truck load of timber is shared amongst the team.

During one week, each team employee worked 40 hours, and the team loaded 9 trucks with timber.

Each team member would earn:

Basic rate	40 hours x £12.00	£480.00
Overtime rate	(9 trucks x £50) / 6 employees	£75.00
Total		£555.00

piecework

Piecework is payment based on the number of items produced by the employee.

Payment by 'piecework' is the name given to labour payments that are entirely based on output or production levels. Unlike the methods that we have examined already, piecework schemes do not take account of the time that the employee spends working. Instead, piecework simply makes a payment per unit produced, and this is the only amount that the employee earns.

worked example

Suppose an employee is paid by piecework based on £15 per unit produced.

During the week the employee works 46 hours and produces 28 units.

The employee will be paid £15 x 28 units = £420.00.

Note that the time spent working is not used in the calculation at all.

For the business, the piecework method means that each unit produced has the same labour cost, and payment is only made for productive work. However, not all production processes are suitable for payment by piecework, because the output of each employee cannot always be measured. Close supervision is also required to ensure that the quality of the output does not suffer if the employees rush to produce more units and earn more money.

When piecework is used, the employees' earnings are limited only by the speed of their work, so there is no theoretical limit to how much they can earn. This is likely to make the employee's pay vary week by week.

■ **guaranteed minimum payment**

Some organisations may use a 'piece rate with guarantee' system. This is where a minimum level of piecework or a fixed amount will be paid, regardless of output. It could help satisfy employees where results were poor through factors outside their control (for example a machine breakdown). This method can also be used to ensure that payments meet UK minimum wage legislation.

We will now use a Case Study to illustrate the calculations involved in the payment methods that we have examined.

Case Study

FASHION WORKS: LABOUR COSTS

situation

Fashion Works is a small company that manufactures clothes. It uses various payment methods for its employees. The following are details of the payment methods for a sample of employees in different departments for a week.

Cutting Department: basic rate + productivity bonus

Employees who work in the cutting department are paid £10.00 per hour for a 35 hour week.

The employees are also paid a bonus if they complete more than 10 items per hour. The bonus is £0.25 per item completed in excess of this number.

Rashid Patel works in the cutting department. During the week he worked 35 hours and completed 365 items.

Sewing Department: piecework payment

The sewing machinists in the sewing department are paid at a piecework rate of £6.00 per completed item. Stephan Schallert is a sewing machinist. During the week he worked for 40 hours and completed 89 items.

Sales Department: basic rate + overtime

All employees in the sales department are paid £12.00 per hour for a basic week of 35 hours. Any overtime worked is paid at a rate of £18.00 per hour. Sara Lee works in the sales department. During the week Sara worked the basic 35 hours.

required

Calculate the gross pay for each of the employees listed above.

solution

Cutting Department
Rashid Patel

Time rate: 35 hours x £10.00		£350.00
Bonus calculation:		
Actual output	365 units	
Expected output (35 hours x 10 units)	350 units	
Excess output that earns bonus	15 units	
Bonus payable 15 units x £0.25		£3.75
Total pay		£353.75

Sewing Department
Stephan Schallert

Piecework rate 89 items x £6.00	£534.00

(Hours worked is not relevant)

Sales Department
Sara Lee

Time rate: basic rate	35 hours x £12.00	£420.00

CLASSIFYING AND CODING LABOUR COSTS

We discovered earlier in this book that labour is one of the three main **elements of cost** (materials, labour and expenses). We also saw that **the nature** of labour costs may be:

- **direct** (part of prime cost) or

- **indirect** (part of production overheads or non-production overheads)

Direct labour costs are the costs of employing those who work directly engaged on production. This includes production operatives, but not supervisors or those not directly involved in producing the output of the organisation.

Indirect labour costs are the costs of employing those in the production area who are not directly involved in production, and the cost of employing those who work in other functions (for example administration or selling and distribution).

The following Case Study is developed from the previous Case Study and uses a coding system to classify:

- the **elements** of cost (materials, labour and expenses)

- the **nature** of costs (direct costs, indirect costs)

Case
Study

FASHION WORKS:
CODING LABOUR COSTS

situation

Fashion Works is a small company that manufactures clothes. The gross pay for three sample employees has already been calculated (see page 108), and is summarised below:

Department	Employee	Gross Pay
Cutting	Rashid Patel	£353.75
Sewing	Stephan Schallert	£534.00
Sales	Sara Lee	£420.00

Coding Policy Manual

This internal document includes the following details:

- Sewing and cutting are production activities

- Each code is made up of three digits:

    - the first digit shows the cost centre or profit centre

    - the second digit shows whether the cost is direct or indirect

    - the third digit is for the element of cost (materials, labour, expenses)

- Extract from cost centre / profit centre list (first digit of code)

    1   Cutting Department (cost centre)

    2   Sewing Department (cost centre)

    3   Administration Department (cost centre)

    4   Sales Department (profit centre)

- Extract from list of 'nature' analysis codes (second digit of code)

    1   Direct

    2   Indirect

- Extract from list of 'element' analysis codes (third digit of code)

  1 Materials

  2 Labour

  3 Expenses

- Example of a code:

Direct materials issued to the cutting department would be coded 111.

required

Show the coding relating to each employee's labour cost.

solution

Department	Employee	Gross Pay	Code
Cutting	Rashid Patel	£353.75	112
Sewing	Stephan Schallert	£534.00	212
Sales	Sara Lee	£420.00	422

BEHAVIOUR OF LABOUR COSTS

In Chapter 3 we explained the principles of **cost behaviour.** We identified three basic ways in which costs can behave. These are:

- **fixed costs** – costs that do not change when the output changes – eg when the number of items produced increases

- **stepped costs** – costs that are fixed when output is within a certain range, but will be at a higher fixed level if output is within a higher range

- **variable costs** – those costs which change as the level of output (or activity level) changes

- **semi-variable costs** – those costs that contain both a fixed element and a variable element

Now that we have examined labour costs in some detail we will identify how they can be classified, using most of the above categories. The table shown below summarises the cost behaviour of the main methods of labour payments.

Cost behaviour:	Fixed costs – these do not change with output	Variable costs – these do change with output	Semi-variable costs – a mix of fixed and variable costs
Example based on labour costs:	Basic rate pay – eg for monthly paid administrative and sales staff	Piecework payments – eg for production workers not on basic rate pay	Basic rate pay topped up by a production-based bonus

We will now return to the situation in the previous Case Study to apply these principles.

FASHION WORKS:
LABOUR COST BEHAVIOUR

situation

Fashion Works is a small company that manufactures clothes. It uses various payment methods for its employees (see previous Case Studies).

The gross pay for various employees has already been calculated, and is shown below.

Cutting Department

Rashid Patel
Time rate: 35 hours x £10.00		£350.00
Production-based bonus payable	15 units x £0.25	£3.75
Total pay		£353.75

Sewing Department

Stephan Schallert
Piecework rate	89 items x £6.00	£534.00

Sales Department

Sara Lee
Time rate: basic rate	35 hours x £12.00	£420.00

required

Draw up a table showing the method of payment and the cost behaviour of the labour cost of each employee.

solution

Employee	Method	Cost behaviour
Rashid Patel	Time-based payment with a production-based bonus	Semi-variable
Stephan Schallert	Piecework	Variable
Sara Lee	Time-based payment (basic rate pay only)	Fixed

Chapter Summary

■ There are several methods of making labour payments. These include time rates (including basic rates and overtime rates), time rates with bonus systems, and piecework rates.

■ Labour costs can be classified and coded based on the categories covered earlier in this book; these include cost and profit centres, direct and indirect costs.

■ Labour costs can usually behave as fixed costs, variable costs, or semi-variable costs, depending on the method of payment.

Key Terms

time rate	the method of remuneration when payment is on the basis of time spent at work; it can be an hourly rate or based on a longer time period
basic rate	a time rate that is applied to the normal contracted work time, and is usually an hourly rate
overtime rate	the rate (normally hourly) paid for time worked in excess of the normal contracted time; it is usually at a higher rate than basic rate
piecework	a payment system when the employee is paid for the work carried out (eg per task or unit); this does not take any account of the time taken
bonus system	a system used in conjunction with another payment method (for example time rate), which provides additional payment for efficient working – eg production that is more than a set level. It can be used for individuals or teams.
guaranteed minimum payment	a system used in conjunction with piecework payments, where the pay cannot fall below a specified level

Activities

5.1 Which **one** of the following is a characteristic of the time-rate method of labour payment?

(a) Pay is linked directly to output

(b) Employees earn a guaranteed level of pay based on attendance

(c) Hard-working employees earn extra on top of basic pay

(d) Pay is calculated as units of output multiplied by the rate per unit

Answer (a) or (b) or (c) or (d)

5.2 Which **one** of the following is a characteristic of the piecework method of labour payment?

(a) Pay is calculated as hours worked multiplied by hourly rate

(b) Employees are paid an hourly rate plus extra for a higher output than agreed

(c) Pay is unaffected by changes in output

(d) Employees are paid on the basis of output

Answer (a) or (b) or (c) or (d)

5.3 Which **one** of the following is a characteristic of the time-rate plus bonus method of labour payment?

(a) Wages are linked to output but a set level of pay is guaranteed

(b) Employees are paid on the basis of output

(c) Employees earn a fixed level of pay

(d) Pay is calculated as units of output multiplied by the rate per unit

Answer (a) or (b) or (c) or (d)

5.4 Identify the following statements as true or false by putting a tick in the relevant column of the table below.

	True	False
Indirect labour costs cannot be identified with the product or service produced		
Direct labour costs paid on a time-rate basis do not vary directly with the level of activity		
Indirect labour costs include the wages of office staff		
Direct labour costs paid on a piecework basis remain fixed at all levels of output		
Indirect labour costs are a variable cost		
Direct labour costs include the wages of factory supervisors		

5.5 Identify the labour payment method by putting a tick in the relevant column of the table below.

Payment method	Time-rate	Piecework	Time-rate plus bonus
Assured amount of pay for time worked, but no extra pay for efficient working			
Assured amount of pay for time worked, plus possible extra pay based on output			
No assured amount of pay, but no limit on earnings as pay based on the production of employees			

5.6 Identify **one** advantage for each labour payment method by putting a tick in the relevant column of the table below.

Payment method	Time-rate	Piecework	Time-rate plus bonus
Each unit of production has the same labour cost and payment is made only for productive work			
Both the employee and the business know in advance how much will be paid			
When the employee works harder than expected, an additional payment is made above the time-rate			

5.7 Vulcan Ltd pays a time-rate of £12 per hour to its direct labour for a standard 34 hour week. Any of the labour force working in excess of 34 hours per week is paid an overtime rate of £16 per hour.

Calculate the basic wage, overtime and gross wage for the two workers in the table below.

Worker	Hours worked	Basic wage £	Overtime £	Gross wage £
J Cassidy	38			
P Olinski	40			

5.8 Clark Ltd uses a piecework method to pay labour in its factory. The rate used is £1.25 per unit produced.

Calculate the gross wage for the week for the two workers in the table below.

Worker	Units produced in week	Gross wage £
T Theaker	344	
K Panayi	428	

5.9 Benson Ltd uses a time-rate method with bonus to pay its direct labour in its factory. The time-rate used is £11 per hour and a worker is expected to produce 8 units an hour; anything over this and the worker is paid a bonus of £0.50 per unit.

Calculate the basic wage, bonus and gross wage for the three workers in the table below.

Worker	Hours worked	Units produced	Basic wage £	Bonus £	Gross wage £
N Allen	32	284			
T Chalabi	36	312			
A McCall	40	310			

5.10 The following table gives pay data for four employees who work in a factory.

Employee number	Hours worked	Units produced
1	41	440
2	35	400
3	38	300
4	40	420

Calculate the gross pay for each employee based on each of the following alternative payment methods and complete the table below.

(a) Time rate of £10.00 per hour for 35 hour week, with any overtime paid at £15 per hour.

(b) Piecework at £0.95 per unit produced.

(c) Time rate of £10.00 per hour for all hours worked, plus a bonus of £0.50 for each unit produced in excess of 10 per hour.

Employee number	Payment methods		
	(a)	(b)	(c)
1	£	£	£
2	£	£	£
3	£	£	£
4	£	£	£

5.11 Country Cottage Doors Limited has a range of employees who are paid by different methods. The normal working hours for each full time employee are 40 hours per week.

Calculate the basic wage (or piecework), overtime or bonus, and gross wage for the four workers in the table below.

Employee	Basic wage or piecework £	Overtime or bonus £	Gross wage £
John Evans (carpenter) – worked 42 hours – paid £15 per hour – overtime at £20 per hour			
Vikram Singh (door polisher) – 12 doors polished – paid £35 per door polished			
Julian Winstone (part time cleaner) – worked 12 hours – paid £11.00 per hour			
Sara Lewinski (office worker) – paid £450 per week			

5.12 Alpha Motors is a garage that sells and services cars. Both sales and servicing are direct activities.

An extract from the company's coding policy manual is as follows:

Each code is made up of three digits:

- the first digit shows the cost centre or profit centre
- the next digit shows whether the cost is direct or indirect
- the next digit shows the element of cost (materials, labour, expenses)

Extract from cost centre / profit centre list (first digit of code):

1   Servicing Department (cost centre)

2   Administration Department (cost centre)

3   Sales Department (profit centre)

Extract from list of analysis codes (second digit of code):

1   Direct

2   Indirect

Extract from list of analysis codes (third digit of code):

1   Materials

2   Labour

3   Expenses

The following employees have pay data for the last week:

- Jane Buchan is a mechanic in the servicing department. She earns £12.00 per hour for a 36 hour week, with overtime paid at £16.00 per hour. Jane worked 39 hours.
- Louis Chowski is also a mechanic in the servicing department with the same pay rates and hours as Jane. He worked 40 hours.
- Jim Wright is a car salesman. He earns a basic £500.00 per week, with a bonus of £40.00 for each car sold. He sold two cars in the week.
- John Rogers is the company administrator. He earns £420.00 per week.

Calculate the gross pay for each employee and show the coding, using the following table.

Employee	Basic pay £	Overtime or bonus £	Total pay £	Code
Jane Buchan				
Louis Chowski				
Jim Wright				
John Rogers				

5.13 At a cake manufacturing factory, the following employees are paid as shown below:

- Bill Brown is a machine operator in the factory and his clock card for last week shows that he worked 38 hours. His hourly rate of pay is £12 per hour.

- Sheila Williams is a skilled nutritionist designing new products and her clock card shows that she worked 44 hours. Her hourly rate of pay is £20 per hour, with overtime for hours worked beyond 40 hours per week at a rate of £25 per hour.

- Sonja Patel is a production supervisor. She is paid a weekly rate of £530 per week.

An extract from the company's coding policy manual is as follows:

Each code is made up of three digits:

- the first digit shows the cost centre

- the next digit shows whether the cost is direct or indirect

- the next digit shows the element of cost (materials, labour, expenses)

Extract from cost centre list:

1   Factory

2   Product design

3   Offices

Extract from list of analysis codes (second digit):

1   Direct

2   Indirect

Extract from list of analysis codes (third digit):

1   Materials

2   Labour

3   Expenses

Calculate the gross pay for each employee and show the coding, using the following table.

Employee	Basic pay £	Overtime £	Total pay £	Code
Bill Brown				
Sheila Williams				
Sonja Patel				

6 Using budgets and calculation tools

this chapter covers...

In this chapter we will examine budgets and the part they play in the management of an organisation. We will describe:

- *how budgets can be used to help monitor and control the costs of an organisation*

- *the difference between fixed and flexible budgets*

- *how to prepare simple budgets*

- *variances – the differences between budgeted and actual costs*

- *the need to be able to identify 'adverse' and 'favourable' variances*

- *the need to be able to identify 'significant' variances based on definitions that are provided*

- *how to identify potential causes and effects of variances*

We will then examine typical reporting structures of organisations, and the importance of being able to decide which manager is likely to require information about variances.

The rest of the chapter is then used to examine how computer-based tools can be used to help calculate and present costing information. This includes how formulas can be used to carry out calculations automatically, and how data can be formatted to make it clearer.

BUDGETS – COMPARING ACTUAL AND EXPECTED INCOME AND COSTS

what is a budget?

A budget is a financial plan for an organisation that is prepared in advance.

A budget is an important part of the planning process that needs to be carried out by managers. It will be based on:

- the products that will be made (or services provided)

- the number of products that will be made (or services provided) and sold, and the expected revenue

A budget will also calculate the expected costs of the organisation, often analysed into the various classifications that we have studied earlier in this book.

what are the purposes of a budget?

The main purposes of a budget are as follows, although organisations may place different emphasis on the various purposes to suit their needs.

- **the budget creates plans**

By producing a budget, managers can ensure that they have achievable plans that have been properly agreed. They will know what they need to do to achieve those plans.

- **the budget communicates and coordinates the plans**

Each manager in the organisation needs to know what the plans are and what their part is in fulfilling these plans. They must all work together using the same overall plan.

- **the budget can be used to monitor and control**

An important reason for producing a budget is so that the actual results can be monitored against the budget. This will enable action to be taken where necessary to achieve the required result.

The key features of a budget that we should remember are that

- the budget helps with **planning**

- it can also be used to **monitor** and **control** what actually happens

It is this concept of **monitoring** and **control** that is very important when managing an organisation.

standard costs

You may come across the term 'standard costs' in relation to a budget. Just like budgeted costs, standard costs are expected costs that have been calculated in advance.

Whereas budgets tend to be used for total income and costs for a period, standard costs are calculated for individual units of output – for example an individual product or service. Not every organisation creates standard costs for their products, but where they are available they can then be used to help create budgets.

You may find that the term 'budgeted / standard costs' (or something similar) is used to describe expected costs in an activity or assessment task. Whatever term is used to describe expected costs, they are used in the same way to make comparisons with actual costs and to calculate variances, as we will see shortly.

fixed and flexible budgets

The usefulness of a budget will depend on how the budgeted output or activity level (eg number of units made and sold) matches what actually happens. There are two types of budget that can be used.

- **Fixed budgets** are used when the output can be accurately predicted in advance, and the budget is based on the income and costs arising from this level of output. The actual income and costs can be compared directly with this budget, and variances calculated, as we shall see shortly.

  An example of a situation when this sort of budget would be suitable would be if there was a contract in place to produce and sell an agreed number of items.

- **Flexible (or flexed) budgets** are used when it is more difficult to predict the output or activity level, and income and costs will depend on this level. In this situation, an initial budget is prepared, which is then adjusted (or flexed) so that it is in line with the actual output or activity level, once it is known. Only when this has happened can the revised budget be used to compare with the actual income and costs. The flexing of the budget would use the cost behaviour techniques that we saw in Chapter 3.

  This type of budget would be suitable in (for example) a restaurant where the number of meals served (and therefore the income and costs) varies in each period.

The following example will show how a flexible budget is prepared, and it will remind us how cost behaviour calculations can be used.

worked example

A company has prepared the following original budget **based on producing and selling 20,000 units** in the period.

	£
Revenue	300,000
Less costs:	
Materials	55,000
Labour	76,000
Fixed overheads	103,000
Profit	66,000

When the period was completed, it was found that only 18,000 units were made and sold. In order to make a fair comparison with the actual income and costs, a flexible budget is to be prepared. This will be based on what the budget would have looked like if the actual activity level had been known. It has been established that revenue is based on output, and that materials and labour are variable costs.

The following flexible budget is based on the **actual output level of 18,000 units**, with notes showing calculations.

	£	
Revenue	270,000	Based on £300,000 / 20,000 = £15 per unit.
Less costs:		
Materials	49,500	Based on £55,000 / 20,000 = £2.75 per unit
Labour	68,400	Based on £76,000 / 20,000 = £3.80 per unit
Fixed overheads	103,000	Unchanged as a fixed cost
Profit	49,100	Recalculated

Note that this lower output level means that the budgeted profit level is lower than the one shown in the original budget. This revised flexed budget can then be used fairly to compare directly with the actual income and costs.

preparing budgets

You may be asked to prepare a budget for a single product organisation. This uses the knowledge about costs that you have developed in earlier chapters, together with some arithmetic. The following Case Study shows how a simple budget can be prepared from estimates and other information provided about a future period.

BUD AND COMPANY:
PREPARING A BUDGET

situation

You are employed in the finance department of Bud and Company, and you have been provided with various data related to the plans for the next year. You have been provided with a template, and you have been asked to use the data to prepare a fixed budget.

The company plans to make and sell 60,000 units in the year, with a selling price of £15 each.

Each unit requires 2 kilos of material. There is a contract in place with the supplier to provide the material for £1.20 per kilo.

Each member of the direct labour force is paid £12 per hour. During an hour an employee can make 3 units.

The fixed overheads for the year are estimated at £395,000.

The following template should be used to prepare the budget.

Bud and Company Budget for 20-5		
	£	£
Revenue		
Materials		
Labour		
Fixed Overheads		
Profit		

required

Prepare the budget for 20-5.

solution

Bud and Company Budget for 20-5		
	£	£
Revenue		900,000
Materials	144,000	
Labour	240,000	
Fixed Overheads	395,000	
Profit		121,000

Workings:

Revenue £15 x 60,000   = £900,000

Materials 2 x £1.20 x 60,000   = £144,000

Labour   (£12 / 3) x 60,000   = £240,000

calculating variances

■ **variances for costs**

In order to monitor and control costs we need to compare actual costs with budgeted costs. We will carry this out for each type of cost, and calculate any differences between the budget figures and the actual figures. These differences are known as **variances** and can be either:

— **adverse** – where the actual cost is greater than the budgeted cost, or

— **favourable** – where the actual cost is less than the budgeted cost.

These descriptions of variances are fairly self-explanatory; adverse variances are 'bad news', whereas favourable variances are 'good news'. These variances for costs are always calculated as:

budgeted cost minus actual cost

If the answer is positive, the variance is favourable; if the answer is negative, the variance is adverse.

worked example

If budgeted material costs for a month were £85,000, but the actual material costs were £93,000, then the material variance would be £8,000 adverse. This is calculated as £85,000 – £93,000 = –£8,000. Notice that the negative answer confirms that it is an adverse variance, although this should be clear from the figures since the actual cost is greater.

■ **variances for income**

When we are calculating the variances for income, if the actual income were greater than budgeted income this would create a favourable variance – ie the calculation would be the other way around.

MONITOR LIMITED:
CALCULATING VARIANCES

situation

You work for Monitor Limited, a company that manufactures speed cameras. The company uses fixed budgets, as it can accurately predict output. One of your duties is to calculate variances based on the monthly variance report of budgeted and actual income and costs. The latest (partly completed) report is shown below.

	Budget £	Actual £	Variance £	Adverse or Favourable
Income	280,000	275,000		
Direct materials	47,500	49,200		
Direct labour	59,800	66,400		
Production overheads	74,200	73,600		
Administration overheads	35,900	36,900		
Selling and distribution overheads	28,400	24,700		

required

Complete the report, showing variances and whether each variance is adverse or favourable.

solution

	Budget £	Actual £	Variance £	Adverse or Favourable
Income	280,000	275,000	5,000	Adverse
Direct materials	47,500	49,200	1,700	Adverse
Direct labour	59,800	66,400	6,600	Adverse
Production overheads	74,200	73,600	600	Favourable
Administration overheads	35,900	36,900	1,000	Adverse
Selling and distribution overheads	28,400	24,700	3,700	Favourable

identifying significant variances

Some variances may be considered **significant** – these are the ones that managers will probably want to investigate most thoroughly. You may be asked to identify (to point out) significant variances, and you would be told how to decide whether any variances were significant or not. There are two main methods of identifying significant variances. Both are quite straightforward, but care is needed in the calculation.

- **Is the variance greater than a given amount?** For example, variances over £5,000 may be considered significant. This could be different for each type of variance – for example adverse variances over £6,000 could be considered significant, but favourable variances might have to be over £8,000.

- **Is the variance greater than a given percentage of the budgeted figure?** For example, a variance greater than 5% of the budget figure could be considered significant. Again, care is needed with the calculation to make sure you are working out a percentage of the budget figure.

calculating percentages of budget figures

When we are presented with actual data and budgeted data, then the variance can be calculated, as we have already seen. To check whether this variance is greater than a given percentage of the budget figure, one method of calculation is to:

1   Divide the variance (ignoring its sign) by the budget figure.

2   Multiply the answer by 100 (or press % on your calculator).

3   Compare this answer with the given percentage.

worked example

Suppose actual direct labour costs for September are £14,720, and the budgeted figure is £14,000. You are asked whether the variance is significant, and told that significant variances are greater than 5% of the budgeted figure.

We firstly calculate the variance as budgeted costs – actual costs.

Variance is £14,000 – £14,720 = minus £720

Then (ignoring the minus sign), divide this figure by the budgeted figure and multiply the answer by 100.

(£720 ÷ £14,000) x 100 = 5.14% (rounded to two decimal places)

This is greater than 5%, so the variance is significant.

Notice that if we had divided the variance by the actual figure by mistake we would have produced an incorrect answer of less than 5%, which would not appear to be significant.

Please note that when carrying out these calculations you will need to read the instructions very thoroughly, and carry out your calculations carefully.

We will now use the data from the last Case Study to identify significant variances.

MONITOR LIMITED:
IDENTIFYING SIGNIFICANT VARIANCES

situation

You have already calculated variances based on comparisons between last month's budgeted and actual costs. Your manager now asks you to identify which of the variances are significant.

He tells you that significant variances are those in excess of 10% of budget. This applies to both favourable and adverse variances.

required

He asks you to:

(a) calculate for each type of cost the percentage of the variance in relation to the budgeted figure, to two decimal places

(b) complete the final column in the performance report by stating whether each variance is 'significant' or 'not significant'

solution

(a) **variance percentage – workings**

Income = $\dfrac{5,000}{280,000} \times 100$ = 1.79%

Direct materials = $\dfrac{1,700}{47,500} \times 100$ = 3.58%

Direct labour = $\dfrac{6,600}{59,800} \times 100$ = 11.04%

Production overheads = $\dfrac{600}{74,200} \times 100$ = 0.81%

Administration overheads = $\dfrac{1,000}{35,900} \times 100$ = 2.79%

Selling and distribution overheads = $\dfrac{3,700}{28,400} \times 100$ = 13.03%

Cost type	Budget £	Actual £	Variance £	Adverse or favourable	Significant or not significant
Income	280,000	275,000	5,000	Adverse	Not significant
Direct materials	47,500	49,200	1,700	Adverse	Not significant
Direct labour	59,800	66,400	6,600	Adverse	Significant
Production overheads	74,200	73,600	600	Favourable	Not significant
Administration overheads	35,900	36,900	1,000	Adverse	Not significant
Selling and distribution overheads	28,400	24,700	3,700	Favourable	Significant

REPORTING TO MANAGERS

In the last section we explained how to calculate variances, and how significant variances may be identified to help managers focus their attention. We must now consider which managers are the most appropriate to report variances to.

While each organisation will have a slightly different structure, we can still consider a typical organisation, and suggest which managers should be reported to.

In addition to cost centre and profit centre managers, other managers will have responsibilities for income and certain costs. The summary on the next page shows some typical responsibilities of managers. Notice that in some cases more than one manager is listed as an alternative.

areas of cost and the managers who are responsible

Income or Cost	Manager responsible
Income	Sales Manager
Materials	Production Manager
	Purchasing Manager
Labour	Production Manager
	Human Resources Manager
Expenses	Administration Manager
Production Overheads	Production Manager
Administration Overheads	Administration Manager
Selling and Distribution Overheads	Sales Manager
	Distribution / Transport Manager
Financial Overheads	Finance Manager
	Company Accountant

We will now continue the previous Case Study and identify the managers for the individual areas of cost.

Case
Study

MONITOR LIMITED:
IDENTIFYING APPROPRIATE MANAGERS

situation

You have already calculated variances, and identified those which are significant. You are now asked to identify the managers who would find the information in your report useful.

required

Complete the performance report by identifying one or more appropriate managers for each category. Enter the details in the right-hand column.

solution

Income or Cost	Variance £	Adverse or favourable	Significant or not significant	Manager
Income	5,000	Adverse	Not significant	Sales Manager
Direct materials	1,700	Adverse	Not significant	Production Manager or Purchasing Manager
Direct labour	6,600	Adverse	Significant	Production Manager or Human Resources Manager
Production overheads	600	Favourable	Not significant	Production Manager
Administration overheads	1,000	Adverse	Not significant	Administration Manager
Selling and distribution overheads	3,700	Favourable	Significant	Sales Manager or Distribution Manager

causes and effects of variances

You may be asked to suggest possible causes of variances, and comment on their effect. If you are provided with information about the situation that you are presented with, then you should use it to help with your answer. For example, if you are told that the labour force received a pay rise that had not been budgeted for, then that is a likely cause of an adverse direct labour variance.

If the organisation is correctly using a fixed or a flexed budget, then the actual output (or activity level) should be in line with the budget. This means that **the output level itself will not be a cause of any variance.**

We will now list some common causes of variances in the form of a table. You may be able to think of other causes.

Income or Cost	Adverse Variances	Favourable Variances
Revenue	Selling price lower than budgeted	Selling price higher than budgeted
Direct materials	Purchase price higher than budgeted More material used than expected	Purchase price lower than budgeted Less material used than expected
Direct labour	Pay rate higher than budgeted (eg pay rise, or more time paid at overtime rates) Work took more time than expected	Pay rate lower than expected (eg planned pay rise postponed) Work carried out more quickly than expected
Overheads	Costs higher than expected – for example: Higher light and heat price or usage Rent increase Indirect staff pay rise Additional indirect staff employed	Costs lower than expected – for example: Lower light and heat price or usage Indirect staff pay rise postponed Fewer indirect staff employed

The effect of variances is that

- adverse variances will result in lower profits
- favourable variances will result in higher profits

There may also be specific effects based on the underlying cause of a particular variance. For example, although a postponed pay rise would lead to a favourable labour variance, it could also result in a disgruntled workforce who would work less efficiently in future.

You may be asked to suggest potential causes or effects of specific variances, and state which manager the issue should be reported to. The following Case Study examines this area.

MONITOR LIMITED:
POTENTIAL CAUSES AND EFFECTS

situation

You have already identified two significant variances for Monitor Limited. (See previous parts of Case Study).

These are:

Direct labour	Adverse	£6,600
Selling and distribution overheads	Favourable	£3,700

You have established the following facts about the period covered by the variances:

*   A material price increase was imposed by a supplier

*   The office administrator received a pay bonus

*   Good weather led to a reduced usage of electricity

*   The Assistant Sales Manager left his job, and was not replaced

*   A pay rise was awarded to production workers that was not budgeted for

required

State which one of the above facts is a potential cause for each significant variance, and what the effect of each significant variance is on profit. Also confirm the relevant manager to whom this should be reported.

solution

Significant Variance	Potential Cause	Effect on Profit	Relevant Manager
Direct labour adverse variance £6,600	A pay rise was awarded to production workers that was not budgeted for	Reduce profit	Production Manager or Human Resources Manager
Selling and distribution overheads favourable variance £3,700	The Assistant Sales Manager left his job, and was not replaced	Increase profit	Sales Manager

USING CALCULATION TOOLS

There are various types of computer software which are useful for costing. One of the most commonly used type is spreadsheets, which contain calculation tools. One spreadsheet is Microsoft 'Excel', but there are others which work in a similar way. You don't need to use any specific software to study this unit.

A spreadsheet has a grid structure, made up of individual 'boxes' called cells. Along the top of the grid are column letters, and down the left side of the grid are row numbers. Each cell is identified by its location. This is done by referring to the column letter (located above the cell), and the row number (located horizontally to the left of the cell).

For example, a cell identified as B5 would be found in the location shown on the following image.

	A	B	C	D	E
1					
2					
3					
4					
5		**Cell B5**			

Each cell can be used to contain numbers or words that the user has inserted manually. It can alternatively be used for the automatic result of a formula that has been set up. We will see how some useful formulas are created a little later in this chapter.

some spreadsheet terms

We have already used the term 'cell' to describe a location in a spreadsheet that may contain numbers or words etc. The following are a few other terms that you may need to understand.

■ Worksheet – this is the name given to each 'page' of a spreadsheet. These pages will often be originally named as simply 'sheet1' etc, but can be easily renamed to suit the user (for example 'direct costs 20-6').

■ Workbook – this is a collection of worksheets which are all held together as one file within the folders held on the computer. The filename is created to suit the user (for example 'budget 20-6') when the spreadsheet is saved.

■ Password – this is a 'word' made up of letters and / or numbers which the user can create to protect the contents of a spreadsheet workbook. The password should only be known to authorised users, and once set up, the workbook can only be opened by keying in the password.

presenting information using a spreadsheet

Much of the information that we use in costing naturally falls into columns and rows. Many of the tables that we used throughout this book are collections of columns and rows, and these could easily be presented by using a spreadsheet. As we will see later, the inclusion of totals for our columns and / or rows is very easy when using a spreadsheet.

When presenting information using a spreadsheet, we need to make sure that it is easy to understand – not just for us, but also for anyone who would need to use it. To do this there are a few simple rules that should be followed.

- The title of the spreadsheet should be clearly stated. This should be an unambiguous form of words that tells the reader what the spreadsheet is all about. 'Budget figures' would not be very helpful, whereas 'Budgeted and Actual Costs December 20-6' would be better. The title would normally be placed across the top of the spreadsheet page. If there are several worksheets, one could be called 'December 20-6' while the filename of the whole spreadsheet might be 'Budgeted and Actual Costs 20-6'.

- Each column should normally have a heading at the top which tells the reader what the data in the column represents. An example would be 'Budget Costs £'. Notice that by putting a £ sign at the top of the column it avoids the need to put one in front of each figure in the column.

- Each horizontal row should also have a description, and this is normally placed to the left of the columns that are used for data. If you are creating a spreadsheet for the first time, make sure that you leave a column for this purpose. The description should be clear and tell the reader what will be found in the horizontal row to the right of the description. An example could be 'Direct Materials'.

- If totals are required these can be placed in a column and / or a row with a suitable heading or description as described above.

The following is a how a spreadsheet page could look. The title has been omitted here for simplicity.

	A	B	C	D	E
1		Budget £	Actual £	Variance £	A / F
2	Direct materials				
3	Direct labour				
4	Overheads				
5	Totals				

You could be required to enter appropriate column headings and / or descriptions of rows as well as data in an examination. The following Case Study provides an example of how such a task could appear.

Case Study

FORMAT LIMITED: INSERTING SPREADSHEET DATA MANUALLY

situation

A company has produced the following cost information for a product:

Variable costs per unit:

Materials	£5
Labour	£4
Fixed costs:	£40,000

A spreadsheet has been partly completed to record the total costs at various production levels.

	A	B	C	D	E
1	Number of units				
2		Total costs £	Total costs £	Total costs £	Total costs £
3	Variable materials				
4	Variable labour	40,000	48,000	60,000	72,000
5	Fixed costs				
6	Totals				

required

(a) Insert column headings into each of the cells B1, C1, D1 and E1 to show the number of units.

(b) Manually insert appropriate figures into the remaining cells.

solution

The first step is to work out how many units should head up each column. This is carried out by dividing each total variable labour cost shown by £4 (the unit variable labour cost).

Next the units are multiplied by the variable material cost per unit to calculate the variable materials cost. The fixed costs are then inserted, and the totals calculated.

	A	B	C	D	E
1	Number of units	10,000	12,000	15,000	18,000
2		Total costs £	Total costs £	Total costs £	Total costs £
3	Variable materials	50,000	60,000	75,000	90,000
4	Variable labour	40,000	48,000	60,000	72,000
5	Fixed costs	40,000	40,000	40,000	40,000
6	Totals	130,000	148,000	175,000	202,000

using basic formulas for calculations

Formulas can be used to automatically calculate the data within a cell. The formula can be entered directly into the cell. As this is carried out, the formula will also appear in the 'formula bar' which is displayed at the top of the spreadsheet page.

Formulas start with the equals sign '=' and can then use cell references together with the following arithmetical and other signs to form an unambiguous instruction for the software.

- Addition: +

- Subtraction: -

- Multiplication: *

- Division   /

An example of a simple formula is:

=F6+F7

which instructs the software to enter into the relevant cell the result of adding the contents of cell F6 to the contents of cell F7.

Formulas can also use numbers in combination with cell references, for example:

=F6*2

which is an instruction to multiply the contents of cell F6 by 2.

Brackets ( ) are also used to instruct the software to deal with the calculation within the brackets first.

For example, if we wish to add together the contents of cells F6 and F7, before multiplying the result by 2 we would use the formula:

=(F6+F7)*2

If the brackets were omitted the software would multiply the contents of cell F7 by 2, and then add the contents of cell F6. This is because the order in which the calculation is carried out is always as follows:

- Firstly – any calculation contained in brackets

- Secondly – any multiplication and / or division

- Thirdly – any addition and / or subtraction

We will now use the previous Case Study to see one way that we could have used formulas for working out the column totals.

FORMAT LIMITED:
USING FORMULAS FOR ADDITION

situation

The following spreadsheet has been created to show total costs of a product at various production levels.

	A	B	C	D	E
1	Number of units	10,000	12,000	15,000	18,000
2		Total costs £	Total costs £	Total costs £	Total costs £
3	Variable materials	50,000	60,000	75,000	90,000
4	Variable labour	40,000	48,000	60,000	72,000
5	Fixed costs	40,000	40,000	40,000	40,000
6	Totals	130,000	148,000	175,000	202,000

required

Show the formulas that could be used in cells B6, C6, D6 and E6 to total the relevant columns.

solution

The formulas are as follows:

Cell B6:   =B3+B4+B5

Cell C6:   =C3+C4+C5

Cell D6:   =D3+D4+D

Cell E6:   =E3+E4+E5

Notice that we are only adding the amounts (in £) shown below row 2. For obvious reasons we are ignoring the number of units in row 1 and the headings in row 2. All the formulas here look similar because we are repeating the same pattern each time.

These are not the only formulas that we could use to get these results. Note that in an examination where there are various formulas that will achieve the same result, marks will be awarded for any valid formula.

The next section examines some alternatives.

'SUM' function

We can use 'functions' that are built into the software to simplify some formulas. The 'SUM' function is used to total the content of a number of cells.

The SUM function is used as follows. The equal sign is followed by 'SUM', and this is followed by brackets containing the cell references to be added. The cell references are separated by commas.

This means that: =SUM(B3,B4,B5)

will give the same result as =B3+B4+B5

Where the cells are in the same column or the same row, the formula can be shortened by using the first and last cell references, with a colon ':' between.

For example: =SUM(B3:B5)

This means that all the cells between B3 and B5 would be included.

This is called a range of cells. This is the preferred way to add up a range of cells, as it is neater, and will adjust if a new row of data is added in between two existing rows.

using formulas for multiplication and division

As we noted earlier, multiplication uses the * sign, and division uses the / sign. For example, =F3*12 would multiply the contents of cell F3 by 12, and =G4/6 would divide the contents of cell G4 by 6. Cell addresses could be used in these formulas instead of numbers where appropriate.

We will now use a Case Study to see how this could be useful in a practical situation.

Case Study

OVERSEE LIMITED: USING FORMULAS FOR ADDITION AND SUBTRACTION

situation
Oversee Limited uses a spreadsheet to present budgeted and actual data and calculate profit and variances. The following spreadsheet has been partly completed.

	A	B	C	D	E
1		Budget £	Actual £	Variance £	A / F
2	Income	130,000	145,000		
3	Direct materials	29,500	31,600		
4	Direct labour	44,100	43,000		
5	Overheads	21,500	24,300		
6	Total costs				
7	Profit				

required
- Enter appropriate formulas using the 'sum' function into cells B6 and C6.
- Enter appropriate formulas into cells B7 and B8.
- Enter appropriate formulas into the cells in column D to calculate variances, so that favourable variances have positive values, and adverse variances are negative.
- Enter A or F into the cells in column E to denote adverse or favourable variances (including for profit).

solution

	A	B	C	D	E
1		Budget £	Actual £	Variance £	A / F
2	Income	130,000	145,000	=C2-B2	F
3	Direct materials	29,500	31,600	=B3-C3	A
4	Direct labour	44,100	43,000	=B4-C4	F
5	Overheads	21,500	24,300	=B5-C5	A
6	Total costs	=SUM(B3:B5)	=SUM(C3:C5)	=B6-C6	A
7	Profit	=B2-B6	=C2-C6	=C7-B7	F

Note that for **income** and **profit variances**, if the actual figure is greater than the budget then this results in a favourable variance. This is achieved by calculating the variance as **actual minus budget** figures.

When calculating variances for costs, the opposite is true, since if the actual figure is less than the budget figure a positive favourable variance occurs. Therefore, **cost variances** are calculated as **budget minus actual** figures.

Note also that the formula in some cells refer to cells which themselves contain formulas. This is quite acceptable.

Note also that the formula for the profit variance refers to cells which themselves contain formulas.

There are other formulas that could be used in this Case Study to achieve the same results.

Case Study

FUNCTION LIMITED: USING MULTIPLICATION AND DIVISION

situation

Function Limited has a section in which four employees work as a team. Each employee is paid a basic £15 for each hour worked. In addition, a team bonus is calculated each week and divided equally among the four employees. The total team bonus is based on £20 for each unit that the team produced in excess of 70 units.

During a specific week the employees had the following data.

Employee	Hours Worked	Units Produced
M. Fletcher	38	
S. Khan	40	
P. Smythe	37	
N. Cathay	40	
Team output		77

The following spreadsheet (partly completed) is used to present the amount of pay for each member of the team.

	A	B	C	D	E	F
1		Team Production (units)	Minimum Production for bonus (units)	Excess Production (units)	Team Bonus per excess unit £	Team Total Bonus £
2	Team Bonus Calculation		70		20	
3		M. Fletcher	S. Khan	P. Smythe	N. Cathay	Team Total
4	Hours Worked					
5	Hourly Rate £	15	15	15	15	
6	Basic Pay £					
7	Bonus £					=F2
8	Total Pay £					

Row 2 is used to calculate the team bonus.

Rows 4 to 8 are used to calculate pay, with appropriate team totals shown in column F.

required

- enter the production data into B2, and suitable formulas into D2 and F2

- enter hours worked into row B4

- enter appropriate formulas into the relevant remaining cells to provide the required information

- show how the spreadsheet would look incorporating the figures that the formulas would calculate

solution

	A	B	C	D	E	F
1		Team Production (units)	Minimum Production for bonus (units)	Excess Production (units)	Team Bonus per excess unit £	Team Total Bonus £
2	Team Bonus Calculation	77	70	=B2-C2	20	=D2*E2
3		M. Fletcher	S. Khan	P. Smythe	N. Cathay	Team Total
4	Hours Worked	38	40	37	40	
5	Hourly Rate £	15	15	15	15	
6	Basic Pay £	=B4*B5	=C4*C5	=D4*D5	=E4*E5	=SUM(B6:E6)
7	Bonus £	=F7/4	=F7/4	=F7/4	=F7/4	=F2
8	Total Pay £	=B6+B7	=C6+C7	=D6+D7	=E6+E7	=SUM(B8:E8)

(The figures which result from these calculations are shown on the next page.)

	A	B	C	D	E	F
1		Team Production (units)	Minimum Production for bonus (units)	Excess Production (units)	Team Bonus per excess unit £	Team Total Bonus £
2	Team Bonus Calculation	77	70	7	20	140
3		M. Fletcher	S. Khan	P. Smythe	N. Cathay	Team Total
4	Hours Worked	38	40	37	40	
5	Hourly Rate £	15	15	15	15	
6	Basic Pay £	570	600	555	600	2,325
7	Bonus £	35	35	35	35	140
8	Total Pay £	605	635	590	635	2,465

Note that in some cases, other formulas could be used to achieve the same results.

formatting data

There are many useful ways that numbers and cells can be formatted to make the data clearer and easier to read. We will describe these techniques by referring to Excel spreadsheets (for example where the icons or menus are found on the screen), but other software will have similar processes.

You are strongly advised to practise using all these formatting tools using spreadsheet software. In the AAT assessment you will be presented with an interactive table simulating a spreadsheet with simple formatting tools. When you reach a suitable stage in your studies you should familiarise yourself with the AAT Practice Assessments which will allow you to see how these will work.

For all these processes, firstly select the cell or cells that you wish this to apply to, then follow the directions below.

■ **Format numbers**

Towards the middle of the top of the screen on the 'Home' tab, you will see a section with the title 'Number' shown below a drop-down menu and a series of symbols or icons. You can use either the drop-down menu, or the icons below it to activate the formats described here.

– Thousand separators

These are the familiar commas that are used so that (for example) the number 26593 would appear as 26,593.

The series of icons includes a large comma. Select this symbol.

- Decimals

  The number of decimal places for numbers can be selected (including whether you wish to show just whole numbers). In the same line of symbols as just described, there is a pair of symbols with a left or right arrow and a decimal point and several zeros. The symbol with the arrow pointing left will increase the number of digits below the decimal point, and the symbol with the arrow pointing right will decrease the number of digits below the decimal point.

- Percentages

  In the same line of symbols, you will find a % sign. By selecting this, the numbers in the cell will automatically be multiplied by 100, and a % sign will be placed after the numbers in the cell. The number of decimal places displayed can be adjusted as in the above.

- Accounting

  By using the drop-down menu that is located just above the symbols that were just described, you can select 'Accounting'. This will assume that the numbers in the selected cell(s) are amounts of money, and it will show £ signs and two decimal places to denote pence. A further drop-down menu is also available (from the money icon showing notes and coin) to change the currency if necessary (eg from £ to $).

■ **Format cells**

Towards the top left of the screen can be found various icons that will allow text etc within cells to be presented differently. You may need to use the following formats.

- Bold

  Within the 'Font' section of the screen is a **B** symbol. Using this will **embolden** the contents of the cell(s). It is useful (for example) for column headings.

- Italics

  This icon is also in the 'Font' section. The symbol is *I* and will show the text in *italics*. It is useful for making some text stand out from the rest.

- Underline

  Also in the 'Font' section, this symbol is an underlined capital <u>U</u>, and selecting it will <u>underline</u> the text in the chosen cell(s). There is also a drop-down menu located next to the icon, where double underlining can be selected.

– Borders

In the 'Font' section, next to the underline icon is an icon with a drop-down menu to select a border around the cell or cells. There is a large variety of border styles to choose from.

– Fill with colour

The next icon in the 'Font' section allows you to fill the selected cell(s) with a background colour. Using the drop-down menu, the chosen colour can be selected from a wide range. The cell can still be used for all the usual data or formulas.

– Text size

In the 'Font' section, just above the icons is a drop-down menu where the size of the text can be selected.

– Wrap text

To the right of the 'Font' section is the 'Alignment' section. This contains the 'Wrap Text' icon. This can be used where the text would otherwise be longer than the cell width. It will automatically put the text into more than one line, within the cell. This may involve making the cell taller (ie deeper).

– Merge

Below the 'Wrap Text' icon, within the 'Alignment' section, is a drop-down menu that allows you to merge cells. To use this feature, select the cells that you wish to be treated as one cell. If you use this for cells that already have data in them, then only the data in the upper-left cell will appear in the merged cell. This should only be used for cells containing text and not for numbers.

■ **Copy and paste cells**

If you wish to copy single or multiple cells (for example a substantial part of a worksheet), then use the 'copy and paste' system. Firstly, select all the cells to be copied. Then select the 'copy' icon from the 'Clipboard' section at the top left of the screen. Finally, select the destination cells, and select the 'paste' icon from the 'Clipboard'. This procedure will maintain the integrity of the whole section of the new copy, by automatically changing the cell addresses of any formulas contained in the copied cells. Note that copy and paste can also be accessed by selecting the appropriate option from the menu displayed when right clicking the cells.

■ **Insert rows and columns**

Towards the right of the menus at the top of the screen is a section named 'Cells'. This contains a drop-down menu to 'Insert'.

To insert a new blank row in your work, select a cell where you want the new row to be, and use the 'Insert Sheet Rows' icon from the drop-down menu. This will move all the rows below your chosen position down one row, and automatically change any cell addresses contained in formulas.

To insert a new blank column in your work, select a cell where you want the new column to be, and use the 'Insert Sheet Columns' icon from the drop-down menu. This will move all the columns to the right of your chosen position across one column to the right, and automatically change any cell addresses contained in formulas.

An alternative way to access this procedure is to select the appropriate option from the menu displayed when right clicking on the column letter or row number.

Chapter Summary

■ A budget is a financial plan for an organisation, prepared in advance. The purposes of a budget include planning, monitoring, and controlling.

■ Budgets may be 'fixed' where output is known in advance or 'flexible' and can be changed to reflect different output levels.

■ Comparisons of actual data with budgeted figures make the actual data more useful for planning and decision making. Differences between actual and budgeted data (called 'variances') can be calculated in monetary and percentage terms, and significant differences can be identified and acted upon.

■ Reporting of variances should be made to the appropriate manager. This is normally the person who has responsibility for the income or costs.

■ There are potential causes and effects of variances that can also be reported to the appropriate manager.

■ Cost calculations can be supported by various computer-based tools and techniques, including using spreadsheets.

■ Spreadsheets can be used to present costing information. The data can be input directly into cells arranged in rows and columns.

■ Formulas can also be used in spreadsheets to make automatic calculations. They can be used for adding, subtracting, multiplying and dividing. Data can also be formatted for ease of use using such software.

Key Terms	**budget**	a financial planning document that is prepared in advance, and can be used to help monitor and control costs
	variances	the difference between the actual data and the budgeted data
	adverse variances	these are 'bad news' – in a performance report when the actual income is lower than budget – in a performance report when the actual cost is higher than budget
	favourable variances	these are 'good news' – in a performance report when the actual cost is lower than budget – in a performance report when the actual income is higher than budget
	significant variance	a variance that is brought to the managers' attention for further investigation due to either its high monetary value or the high percentage of the variance from the budget data
	fixed budget	a budget based on one output level, used where the level is known in advance
	flexible budget	a budget that can be adapted to align with the actual output level, once it is known
	spreadsheet	computer software that provides a grid structure that can be used for inputting data and formulas
	cell	a single 'box' on a spreadsheet that can contain data
	worksheet	one page of a spreadsheet file
	workbook	a collection of spreadsheet worksheets that is held as a single file
	formula	an instruction contained within a cell to carry out a calculation
	formatting data	various ways that the use or appearance of spreadsheet data can be modified to help the user

Activities

6.1 A manufacturer has the following cost information for a production level of 20,000 units:

Direct materials	12,000 kilos at £25 per kilo
Direct labour	4,000 hours at £10 per hour
Indirect expenses	£60,000 in total

Calculate the unit costs by element and in total, using the following table.

Element	Total cost (20,000 units) £	Unit cost £
Materials		
Labour		
Expenses		
Total		

6.2 A company is costing a single product, and has the following information available:

Variable costs per unit:

Materials	£8
Labour	£5
Total fixed costs	£60,000

The production level may be 10,000 units, or it may be 15,000.

Complete the following table.

	10,000 units		15,000 units	
	Total cost £	Unit cost £	Total cost £	Unit cost £
Materials				
Labour				
Fixed Costs				
Total				

6.3 Lynx Ltd makes a single product and for a production level of 24,000 units has the following costs:

Material 6,000 kilos at £20 per kilo

Labour 8,000 hours at £12 an hour

Overheads £48,000

Complete the table below to show the unit cost at the production level of 24,000 units.

Element	Unit cost £
Material	
Labour	
Overheads	
Total	

6.4 Mason Ltd makes a single product and for a production level of 12,000 units has the following costs:

Material 10,000 kilos at £6 per kilo

Labour 7,200 hours at £10 an hour

Overheads £48,000

Complete the table below to show the unit cost at the production level of 12,000 units.

Element	Unit cost £
Material	
Labour	
Overheads	
Total	

6.5 Identify the following statements as being true or false by putting a tick in the relevant column of the table below.

	True	False
An adverse cost variance means budgeted costs are greater than actual costs		
A variance is the difference between budgeted and actual income or cost		

6.6 Identify the following statements as being true or false by putting a tick in the relevant column of the table below.

	True	False
A favourable cost variance means budgeted costs are less than actual costs		
If actual costs are greater than budgeted costs the variance is adverse		

6.7 Unicorn Ltd has produced a performance report detailing budgeted and actual income and costs for last month.

Calculate the amount of the variance for each income and cost and then determine whether it is adverse or favourable by putting a tick in the relevant column of the table below.

Income or cost	Budget £	Actual £	Variance £	Adverse	Favourable
Sales	193,000	191,200			
Direct materials	45,400	50,200			
Direct labour	28,700	28,200			
Production overheads	19,300	20,200			
Administration overheads	6,800	6,700			
Selling and distribution overheads	8,700	9,200			

6.8 Caldwell Ltd has produced a performance report detailing budgeted and actual income and costs for last month.

Calculate the amount of the variance for each income and cost and then determine whether it is adverse or favourable by putting a tick in the relevant column of the table below.

Cost type	Budget £	Actual £	Variance £	Adverse	Favourable
Sales	70,000	72,300			
Direct materials	15,400	14,900			
Direct labour	20,300	21,200			
Production overheads	11,100	10,700			
Administration overheads	7,600	7,800			
Selling and distribution overheads	4,900	4,600			

6.9 The following performance report for last month has been produced for Hamblin Ltd as summarised in the table below. Any variance in excess of 5% of budget is considered to be significant and should be reported to the relevant manager for review and appropriate action.

Examine the variances in the table below and indicate whether they are significant or not significant by putting a tick in the relevant column.

Cost type	Budget £	Variance £	Adverse/ Favourable	Significant	Not significant
Direct materials	40,000	2,500	Adverse		
Direct labour	27,500	1,250	Favourable		
Production overheads	21,000	1,000	Adverse		
Administration overheads	7,500	500	Adverse		
Selling and distribution overheads	6,500	750	Favourable		

6.10 The following performance report for last month has been produced for Waring Ltd as summarised in the table below. Any variance in excess of 10% of budget is deemed to be significant and should be reported to the relevant manager for review and appropriate action.

(a) Examine the variances in the table below and indicate whether they are significant or not significant by putting a tick in the relevant column.

Cost type	Budget £	Variance £	Adverse/ Favourable	Significant	Not significant
Direct materials	84,000	8,000	Adverse		
Direct labour	53,000	2,500	Favourable		
Production overheads	26,500	3,000	Adverse		
Administration overheads	12,500	1,500	Adverse		
Selling and distribution overheads	15,500	1,000	Favourable		

(b) The following table shows possible causes for the **above** variances that have been suggested by an inexperienced trainee. Select those that are correct potential causes for the variances shown above.

Cost type	Suggested cause for variance shown	
Direct materials	Material price increase by supplier	
Direct labour	Unexpected high level of overtime worked	
Production overheads	Unplanned repairs needed to factory roof	
Administration overheads	Reduced cost of broadband contract	
Selling and distribution overheads	Unexpected increase in cost of diesel used by delivery vehicles	

6.11 Hardy Ltd has produced a performance report detailing budgeted and actual costs for last month.

Complete the table below by:

- calculating the amount of the variance for each cost type

- determining whether the variance is adverse or favourable

- determining whether the variance is significant or not significant

For Hardy Ltd significant variances are those in excess of 5% of budget.

Cost type	Budget £	Actual £	Variance £	Adverse/ Favourable	Significant/ Not significant
Direct materials	68,500	64,200			
Direct labour	39,100	40,800			
Production overheads	34,700	33,600			
Administration overheads	45,900	51,000			
Selling and distribution overheads	28,000	25,100			

6.12 A business has a significant variance for direct materials. Which **two** managers should be advised of this?

(a)   Distribution Manager; Production Manager

(b)   Human Resources Manager; Sales Manager

(c)   Production Manager; Purchasing Manager

(d)   Finance Manager; Distribution Manager

Answer (a) or (b) or (c) or (d)

6.13 A business has a significant variance for direct labour. Which **two** managers should be advised of this?

(a)   Distribution Manager; Sales Manager

(b)   Production Manager; Purchasing Manager

(c)   Sales Manager; Human Resources Manager

(d)   Production Manager; Human Resources Manager

Answer (a) or (b) or (c) or (d)

6.14 Suggest managers who should be notified about variances regarding the following costs. Complete the following table.

Type of cost	Responsible Manager
Direct materials	
Production labour	
Production overheads	
Sales Department salaries	
Loan interest	

6.15 You are employed in a clothing manufacturing company, and as part of your accounts training you are required to carry out some exercises to test your knowledge of costing.

You have been asked to complete the following table, based on costs incurred within your company. You are required to:

(a) In the column headed 'element' state whether the cost is for materials, labour, or expense

(b) In the column headed 'direct or indirect' state whether the cost is direct, or indirect

(c) In the column headed 'cost behaviour' state whether costs behave as fixed, variable, or semi-variable costs

Cost	Element	Direct or Indirect	Cost behaviour
Cloth for making dresses			
Production supervisor, who is paid a fixed salary			
Sewing machinist, who is paid on a piecework basis			
Vehicle insurance for delivery vehicle			
Fuel for delivery vehicle			
Power for sewing machines, charged at a flat rate, plus an amount per unit of power			
Sales person, who is paid a basic amount plus sales commission			
Royalties paid to clothing designer			

6.16 A company has produced the following partial cost information for a product:

Variable costs per unit:

    Materials   £8

    Labour   £2

A spreadsheet has been partly completed to record the total costs at various production levels.

	A	B	C	D	E
1	Number of units	Variable Materials £	Variable Labour £	Fixed Costs £	Total Costs £
2			20,000	50,000	
3		120,000			
4			40,000		
5		200,000		50,000	

required

- Insert the number of units into each of the cells A2, A3, A4 and A5.

- Insert appropriate figures into the remaining cells in columns B, C and D.

- Insert appropriate formulas into the cells in column E.

6.17 A company has produced the following cost information for a product:

Variable costs per unit:

Materials	£10
Labour	£5
Fixed costs:	£28,000

A spreadsheet has been partly completed to automatically record the total costs at various production levels.

	A	B	C	D	E
1	Number of units	Variable Materials £	Variable Labour £	Fixed Costs £	Total Costs £
2	5,000				
3	7,500				
4	10,000				

Complete the spreadsheet using **only formulas in all cells.**

6.18 Manage Limited uses a spreadsheet to present budgeted and actual data and calculate profit and variances. The following spreadsheet has been partly completed.

	A	B	C	D	E
1		Budget £	Actual £	Variance £	A / F
2	Revenue	210,000	206,000		
3	Materials	44,500	44,600		
4	Labour	63,100	62,000		
5	Overheads	70,500	74,300		
6	Profit				

required

• Enter A or F into each cell in column E to denote adverse or favourable variances.

• Enter appropriate formulas into the cells in column D to calculate variances, and into the remaining cells in row 6 to calculate profit.

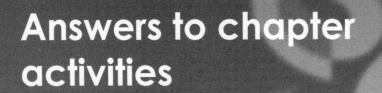

Answers to chapter activities

CHAPTER 1: THE COSTING SYSTEM

1.1   (d)   Financial accounting includes bookkeeping; management accounting includes costing

1.2   (c)   Its purpose is to provide information for owners and investors

1.3   (a)   It is based on future events

1.4

	True	False
Management accounting must comply with company law		✓
Financial accounting provides information for owners and investors	✓	
Management accounting is based on future events	✓	
Financial accounting only provides information about what may happen in the future		✓

1.5

Characteristic	Financial Accounting	Management Accounting
It is based on future events		✓
Its purpose is to provide information for managers		✓
It complies with accounting rules	✓	
It is based on past events	✓	

1.6

Cost	Material	Labour	Overheads
Tubular steel	✓		
Wages of employee operating the moulding machine which produces the chair seats		✓	
Rates of factory			✓
Travel expenses of sales staff			✓
Plastic for making chair seats	✓		
Factory heating and lighting			✓

1.7

Cost	Direct	Indirect
Flour used to bake bread	✓	
Rent of bakery		✓
Wages of bakers	✓	
Repairs to baking machinery		✓
Currants used in buns	✓	
Wages of bakery cleaner		✓
Insurance of bakery		✓
Salary of production manager		✓

1.8

Cost	Production	Administration	Selling and distribution
Wages of employees working on the bottling line	✓		
Insurance of delivery lorries			✓
Cost of bottles	✓		
Safety goggles for bottling line employees	✓		
Advertisement for new employees		✓	
Depreciation of bottling machinery	✓		
Depreciation of sales staff's cars			✓
Attendance at a trade exhibition			✓
Office heating and lighting		✓	
Sales staff salaries			✓

1.9

	Production ('factory') costs		Non-production ('warehouse & office') costs		
	Direct costs	Indirect costs	Administration Indirect costs	Selling and Distribution Indirect costs	Finance Indirect costs
Materials	3	9	11	12	
Labour	2	5	10	8	
Expenses		1	7	4	6

1.10

	True	False
Budgets can never be used as a source of data for historical costs	✓	
Information to help with future costs can come from inside and outside the organisation	✓	
Future costs are impossible to estimate		✓
Financial accounting records and the documents that back up these records are a good source of data for historic costs	✓	
If you have a firm quotation from a supplier this is a good source of data for current costs	✓	
The number of products that the business forecasts to sell is a good source of data for estimating future income	✓	
Costing can only be used for manufacturing businesses, not the service industry		✓
Financial accounts can provide a reliable source of data for future costs		✓
When costing a future product the labour cost may need to be estimated by using planned labour rates and expected times to make the product	✓	
The production level that is planned for is not relevant for costing purposes		✓

CHAPTER 2: COST CENTRES AND OVERHEAD ABSORPTION

2.1   (b)   Frame Construction; Glazing; Administration; Distribution

2.2

Transaction	Code
Sales in Beachside shop	B100
Cost of paying wages of shop staff at Clifftop	C300
Purchase of new display shelving for Beachside	B900
Purchase of goods for resale at Clifftop shop	C200
Cost of electricity at Clifftop shop	C400
Cost of paying wages of company administrator	A300

2.3

Cost	Code
Wages of drivers	B100
Loss in value (depreciation) of vehicles	C200
Fuel for vehicles	A100
Rent of premises	C200
Wages of maintenance staff	B200
Advanced driving courses	C200

2.4

Transaction	Code
Sales invoice showing the sale of £14,750 of academic textbooks to Orton Book Wholesalers Limited	20/420
Printer's bill of £22,740 for printing sports books	50/110
Payroll summary showing overtime of £840 last month in the children's book section	40/220
Payment of £1,540 for advertising sports books in the magazine 'Sport Today'	50/370
Telephone bill of £1,200 for the administration department	60/340
Royalties of £88,245 paid to children's book authors	40/310
Sales invoice showing the sale of £1,890 of novels to the Airport Bookshop	30/410

2.5

Transaction	Code
Wages of the carpenter who assembles the doors	112
Sandpaper	221
Saw sharpening service	123
Wages of the cleaner who works in the door sanding and polishing section	222
Office telephone costs	323
Wood for manufacturing doors	111
Wages of office worker	322

2.6

Overhead absorption method	Units of output £	Direct labour hours £	Machine hours £
Overhead absorption rate	4.00	4.80	12.00
Product A costs:			
Direct materials	11.00	11.00	11.00
Direct labour	30.00	30.00	30.00
Overheads	4.00	14.40	24.00
Total costs	45.00	55.40	65.00

- The Units of output method is least likely to be appropriate for this company. This is because it makes a variety of products and if this method was used, each would bear identical amounts of overhead which is unlikely to be fair.

2.7

Overhead absorption method	Direct labour hours £	Machine hours £
Overhead absorption rate	3.3903	3.7087
Product Q costs:		
Direct materials	21.60	21.60
Direct labour	33.00	33.00
Overheads	10.17	9.27
Total costs	64.77	63.87

2.8

	Budgeted indirect costs	Budgeted direct labour hours	Overhead absorption rate
	£		£
Fabrication	135,600	44,500	3.05
Assembly	101,350	31,900	3.18

Product M	Direct labour hours per unit	Overhead absorption rate	Overhead absorbed
		£	£
Fabrication	4.00	3.05	12.20
Assembly	1.75	3.18	5.57
Total			17.77

CHAPTER 3: COST BEHAVIOUR

3.1

	True	False
Variable costs always include a time period cost		✓
Fixed costs are based on a time period and the amount does not depend on output	✓	
Semi-variable costs change directly with changes in the level of activity		✓

3.2

	True	False
A variable cost is based on a unit of output and is the same for each one	✓	
A fixed cost changes with changes in the level of activity		✓
A semi-variable cost is based on a combination of a time period cost and a per unit cost	✓	

3.3

Costs	Fixed	Variable
Rent of premises	✓	
Labour paid per unit produced		✓
Staff salaries	✓	
Packaging materials for goods produced		✓

3.4

Costs	Fixed	Variable
Insurance of vehicles	✓	
Heating and lighting	✓	
Materials used in production		✓
Bonus paid to production workers for each extra unit of output		✓

3.5

Costs	Fixed	Variable	Semi-variable
Factory rates	✓		
Power for saw and sanders in factory (charged per unit of electricity)		✓	
Factory supervisors' wages (paid a time rate plus a production-based bonus)			✓
Wood used in the production process		✓	
Telephone (charged at a flat rate plus an amount per call)			✓
Office rent	✓		
Polish for finishing doors		✓	
Delivery drivers' pay (paid a time rate plus a bonus per door delivered)			✓
Factory lighting	✓		
Wages of production staff who are paid according to the number of doors they make		✓	
Salary of marketing manager	✓		

3.6

Output (units)	Fixed costs £	Variable costs £	Total costs £	Unit cost £
1,000	30,000	20,000	50,000	50
1,500	30,000	30,000	60,000	40
2,000	30,000	40,000	70,000	35
3,000	30,000	60,000	90,000	30

3.7

Output (units)	Fixed costs £	Variable costs £	Total costs £	Unit cost £
2,000	12,000	4,000	16,000	8
3,000	12,000	6,000	18,000	6
4,000	12,000	8,000	20,000	5
6,000	12,000	12,000	24,000	4

3.8

Output (units)	Stepped costs £	Variable costs £	Total costs £	Unit cost £.p
500	8,000	2,000	10,000	20.00
1,000	8,000	4,000	12,000	12.00
2,000	10,000	8,000	18,000	9.00
4,000	10,000	16,000	26,000	6.50

3.9

	Total cost £	Unit cost £
Material	125,000	5
Labour	100,000	4
Overheads	50,000	2
Total	275,000	11

3.10

	Total cost £	Unit cost £
Material	300,000	10
Labour	240,000	8
Overheads	90,000	3
Total	630,000	21

CHAPTER 4: INVENTORY VALUATION AND THE MANUFACTURING ACCOUNT

4.1

Inventory item and organisation	Classification
Wood held by a door manufacturer	raw materials
Flour held by a cake manufacturer	raw materials
Cakes awaiting icing held by a cake manufacturer	work-in-progress
Doors awaiting sanding and polishing held by a door manufacturer	work-in-progress
Flour held by a flour miller	finished goods
Wheat held by a flour miller	raw materials
Screws held by a screw manufacturer	finished goods
Screws held by a door manufacturer	raw materials

4.2

Characteristic	FIFO	LIFO	AVCO
Issues of inventory are valued at the weighted average cost of purchases			✓
Inventory is valued at the oldest purchase costs		✓	
Issues of inventory are valued at the most recent purchase prices		✓	
Inventory is valued at the weighted average cost of purchases			✓
Inventory is valued at the most recent purchase costs	✓		
Issues of inventory are valued at the oldest purchase prices	✓		

4.3

	True	False
FIFO costs issues of inventory in the same order in which they were received	✓	
FIFO values closing inventory based on the oldest purchase prices		✓
LIFO costs issues of inventory at the oldest purchase prices		✓
LIFO values closing inventory at the average cost of purchases		✓
AVCO costs issues of inventory at the most recent purchase prices		✓
AVCO values closing inventory at the weighted average cost of purchases	✓	

4.4 (d) Inventory balance is valued at the most recent purchase prices

4.5 (a) The latest purchase costs are used to value issues

4.6 (b) Inventory balance is valued at the average of the cost of purchases

4.7 (d) Opening inventory, plus purchases, minus issues, equals closing inventory

4.8 AVCO

4.9

Method	Cost of issue on 26 February £	Closing inventory value at 28 February £
FIFO	2,300	4,400
LIFO	2,900	3,800
AVCO	2,580	4,120

4.10

Method	Cost of issue on 22 January £	Closing inventory value at 31 January £
FIFO	1,600	7,700
LIFO	2,000	7,300
AVCO	1,800	7,500

4.11 **(a)** FIFO

Receipts			Issues			Balance		
Quantity (units)	Cost per unit	Total cost	Quantity (units)	Value per unit	Total value	Quantity (units)	Value per unit	Total value
						2,000	£2.02	£4,040
10,000	£2.20	£22,000				2,000	£2.02	£4,040
						10,000	£2.20	£22,000
						———		———
						12,000		£26,040
			2,000	£2.02	£4,040			
			6,000	£2.20	£13,200			
			———		———			
			8,000		£17,240	4,000	£2.20	£8,800

(b) LIFO

Receipts			Issues			Balance		
Quantity (units)	Cost per unit	Total cost	Quantity (units)	Value per unit	Total value	Quantity (units)	Value per unit	Total value
						2,000	£2.02	£4,040
10,000	£2.20	£22,000				2,000	£2.02	£4,040
						10,000	£2.20	£22,000
						_____		_____
						12,000		£26,040
						2,000	£2.02	£4,040
						2,000	£2.20	£4,400
						_____		_____
			8,000	£2.20	£17,600	4,000		£8,440

(c) AVCO

Receipts			Issues			Balance		
Quantity (units)	Cost per unit	Total cost	Quantity (units)	Value per unit	Total value	Quantity (units)	Value per unit	Total value
						2,000	£2.02	£4,040
10,000	£2.20	£22,000				12,000	£2.17	£26,040
			8,000	£2.17	£17,360	4,000	£2.17	£8,680

4.12

Statement	True
The order was placed at the correct inventory level	
The order was placed early	✓
The order was placed late	
The amount ordered was correct	
The amount ordered was too much	
The amount ordered was too little	✓
The delivery arrived when the inventory reached the buffer level	
The delivery arrived when the inventory was above the buffer level	✓
The delivery arrived when the inventory was below the buffer level	

4.13

	£		£
DIRECT COST	79,000	Opening inventory of raw materials	13,000
Opening inventory of raw materials	13,000	Purchases of raw materials	47,000
Direct labour	30,000	Closing inventory of raw materials	11,000
Closing inventory of finished goods	14,000	DIRECT MATERIALS USED	49,000
COST OF GOODS SOLD	93,000	Direct labour	30,000
Purchases of raw materials	47,000	DIRECT COST	79,000
Opening inventory of finished goods	15,000	Manufacturing overheads	20,000
MANUFACTURING COST	99,000	MANUFACTURING COST	99,000
Closing inventory of work-in-progress	19,000	Opening inventory of work-in-progress	12,000
Opening inventory of work-in-progress	12,000	Closing inventory of work-in-progress	19,000
Closing inventory of raw materials	11,000	COST OF GOODS MANUFACTURED	92,000
DIRECT MATERIALS USED	49,000	Opening inventory of finished goods	15,000
Manufacturing overheads	20,000	Closing inventory of finished goods	14,000
COST OF GOODS MANUFACTURED	92,000	COST OF GOODS SOLD	93,000

4.14

	£		£
Closing inventory of finished goods	32,000	Opening inventory of raw materials	15,000
COST OF GOODS SOLD	178,000	Purchases of raw materials	85,000
Manufacturing overheads	38,000	Closing inventory of raw materials	18,000
Opening inventory of raw materials	15,000	DIRECT MATERIALS USED	82,000
DIRECT MATERIALS USED	82,000	Direct labour	55,000
Opening inventory of work-in-progress	26,000	DIRECT COST	137,000
Direct labour	55,000	Manufacturing overheads	38,000
MANUFACTURING COST	175,000	MANUFACTURING COST	175,000
Opening inventory of finished goods	37,000	Opening inventory of work-in-progress	26,000
COST OF GOODS MANUFACTURED	173,000	Closing inventory of work-in-progress	28,000
Purchases of raw materials	85,000	COST OF GOODS MANUFACTURED	173,000
Closing inventory of work-in-progress	28,000	Opening inventory of finished goods	37,000
DIRECT COST	137,000	Closing inventory of finished goods	32,000
Closing inventory of raw materials	18,000	COST OF GOODS SOLD	178,000

CHAPTER 5: LABOUR COSTS

5.1   (b)   Employees earn a guaranteed level of pay based on attendance

5.2   (d)   Employees are paid on the basis of output

5.3   (a)   Wages are linked to output but a set level of pay is guaranteed

5.4

	True	False
Indirect labour costs cannot be identified with the product or service produced	✓	
Direct labour costs paid on a time-rate basis do not vary directly with the level of activity	✓	
Indirect labour costs include the wages of office staff	✓	
Direct labour costs paid on a piecework basis remain fixed at all levels of output		✓
Indirect labour costs are a variable cost		✓
Direct labour costs include the wages of factory supervisors		✓

5.5

Payment method	Time-rate	Piecework	Time-rate plus bonus
Assured amount of pay for time worked, but no extra pay for efficient working	✓		
Assured amount of pay for time worked, plus possible extra pay based on output			✓
No assured amount of pay, but no limit on earnings as pay based on the production of employees		✓	

5.6

Payment method	Time-rate	Piecework	Time-rate plus bonus
Each unit of production has the same labour cost and payment is made only for productive work		✓	
Both the employee and the business know in advance how much will be paid	✓		
When the employee works harder than expected an additional payment is made above the time-rate			✓

5.7

Worker	Hours worked	Basic wage £	Overtime £	Gross wage £
J Cassidy	38	408	64	472
P Olinski	40	408	96	504

5.8

Worker	Units produced in week	Gross wage £
T Theaker	344	430
K Panayi	428	535

5.9

Worker	Hours worked	Units produced	Basic wage £	Bonus £	Gross wage £
N Allen	32	284	352	14	366
T Chalabi	36	312	396	12	408
A McCall	40	310	440	0	440

5.10

Employee number	Payment methods		
	(a)	(b)	(c)
1	£440	£418	£425
2	£350	£380	£375
3	£395	£285	£380*
4	£425	£399	£410

* no bonus

5.11

Employee	Basic wage or piecework £	Overtime or bonus £	Gross wage £
John Evans (carpenter) – worked 42 hours – paid £15 per hour – overtime at £20 per hour	600	40	640
Vikram Singh (door polisher) – 12 doors polished – paid £35 per door polished	420	0	420
Julian Winstone (part time cleaner) – worked 12 hours – paid £11.00 per hour	132	0	132
Sara Lewinski (office worker) – paid £450 per week	450	0	450

5.12

Employee	Basic pay £	Overtime or bonus £	Total pay £	Code
Jane Buchan	432	48	480	112
Louis Chowski	432	64	496	112
Jim Wright	500	80	580	312
John Rogers	420	0	420	222

5.13

Employee	Basic pay £	Overtime £	Total pay £	Code
Bill Brown	456	0	456	112
Sheila Williams	800	100	900	222
Sonja Patel	530	0	530	122

CHAPTER 6: USING BUDGETS AND CALCULATION TOOLS

6.1

Element	Total cost (20,000 units) £	Unit cost £
Materials	300,000	15
Labour	40,000	2
Expenses	60,000	3
Total	400,000	20

6.2

	10,000 units		15,000 units	
	Total cost £	**Unit cost £**	**Total cost £**	**Unit cost £**
Materials	80,000	8	120,000	8
Labour	50,000	5	75,000	5
Fixed costs	60,000	6	60,000	4
Total	190,000	19	255,000	17

6.3

Element	Unit cost £
Material	5
Labour	4
Overheads	2
Total	11

6.4

Element	Unit cost £
Material	5
Labour	6
Overheads	4
Total	15

6.5

	True	False
An adverse cost variance means budgeted costs are greater than actual costs		✓
A variance is the difference between budgeted and actual income or cost	✓	

6.6

	True	False
A favourable cost variance means budgeted costs are less than actual costs		✓
If actual costs are greater than budgeted costs the variance is adverse	✓	

6.7

Income or cost	Budget £	Actual £	Variance £	Adverse	Favourable
Sales	193,000	191,200	1,800	✓	
Direct materials	45,400	50,200	4,800	✓	
Direct labour	28,700	28,200	500		✓
Production overheads	19,300	20,200	900	✓	
Administration overheads	6,800	6,700	100		✓
Selling and distribution overheads	8,700	9,200	500	✓	

6.8

Income or cost	Budget £	Actual £	Variance £	Adverse	Favourable
Sales	70,000	72,300	2,300		✓
Direct materials	15,400	14,900	500		✓
Direct labour	20,300	21,200	900	✓	
Production overheads	11,100	10,700	400		✓
Administration overheads	7,600	7,800	200	✓	
Selling and distribution overheads	4,900	4,600	300		✓

6.9

Cost type	Budget £	Variance £	Adverse/ Favourable	Significant	Not significant
Direct materials	40,000	2,500	Adverse	✓	
Direct labour	27,500	1,250	Favourable		✓
Production overheads	21,000	1,000	Adverse		✓
Administration overheads	7,500	500	Adverse	✓	
Selling and distribution overheads	6,500	750	Favourable	✓	

6.10

(a)

Cost type	Budget £	Variance £	Adverse/ Favourable	Significant	Not significant
Direct materials	84,000	8,000	Adverse		✓
Direct labour	53,000	2,500	Favourable		✓
Production overheads	26,500	3,000	Adverse	✓	
Administration overheads	12,500	1,500	Adverse	✓	
Selling and distribution overheads	15,500	1,000	Favourable		✓

(b)

Cost type	Suggested cause for variance shown	
Direct materials	Material price increase by supplier	✓
Direct labour	Unexpected high level of overtime worked	
Production overheads	Unplanned repairs needed to factory roof	✓
Administration overheads	Reduced cost of broadband contract	
Selling and distribution overheads	Unexpected increase in cost of diesel used by delivery vehicles	

6.11

Cost type	Budget £	Actual £	Variance £	Adverse/ Favourable	Significant /Not significant
Direct materials	68,500	64,200	4,300	Favourable	Significant
Direct labour	39,100	40,800	1,700	Adverse	Not significant
Production overheads	34,700	33,600	1,100	Favourable	Not significant
Administration overheads	45,900	51,000	5,100	Adverse	Significant
Selling and distribution overheads	28,000	25,100	2,900	Favourable	Significant

6.12 (c) Production Manager; Purchasing Manager

6.13 (d) Production Manager; Human Resources Manager

6.14

Type of cost	Responsible Manager
Direct materials	Purchasing Manager Production Manager
Production labour	Production Manager Human Resources Manager
Production overheads	Production Manager
Sales Department salaries	Sales Manager Human Resources Manager
Loan interest	Finance Manager Company Accountant

6.15

Cost	Element	Direct or Indirect	Cost behaviour
Cloth for making dresses	Material	Direct	Variable
Production supervisor, who is paid a fixed salary	Labour	Indirect	Fixed
Sewing machinist, who is paid on a piecework basis	Labour	Direct	Variable
Vehicle insurance for delivery vehicle	Expense	Indirect	Fixed
Fuel for delivery vehicle	Material	Indirect	Variable
Power for sewing machines, charged at a flat rate, plus an amount per unit of power	Expense	Indirect	Semi-variable
Sales person, who is paid a basic amount plus sales commission	Labour	Indirect	Semi-variable
Royalties paid to clothing designer	Expense	Direct	Variable

6.16

	A	B	C	D	E
1	Number of units	Variable Materials £	Variable Labour £	Fixed Costs £	Total Costs £
2	10,000	80,000	20,000	50,000	=SUM(B2:D2)
3	15,000	120,000	30,000	50,000	=SUM(B3:D3)
4	20,000	160,000	40,000	50,000	=SUM(B4:D4)
5	25,000	200,000	50,000	50,000	=SUM(B5:D5)

Other valid formulas could be used.

6.17

	A	B	C	D	E
1	Number of units	Variable Materials £	Variable Labour £	Fixed Costs £	Total Costs £
2	5,000	=A2*10	=A2*5	=28,000	=SUM(B2:D2)
3	7,500	=A3*10	=A3*5	=28,000	=SUM(B3:D3)
4	10,000	=A4*10	=A4*5	=28,000	=SUM(B4:D4)

Other valid formulas could be used.

6.18

	A	B	C	D	E
1		Budget £	Actual £	Variance £	A / F
2	Revenue	210,000	206,000	=C2-B2	A
3	Materials	44,500	44,600	=B3-C3	A
4	Labour	63,100	62,000	=B4-C4	F
5	Overheads	70,500	74,300	=B5-C5	A
6	Profit	=B2-B3-B4-B5	=C2-C3-C4-C5	=C6-B6	A

Other valid formulas could be used.

Index

for your notes

for your notes

for your notes

for your notes

for your notes

for your notes

for your notes

for your notes

for your notes